CAROLS FOR CHOIRS 1

FIFTY CHRISTMAS CAROLS

Edited and arranged by

REGINALD JACQUES

AND

DAVID WILLCOCKS

MUSIC DEPARTMENT

OXFORD UNIVERSITY PRESS

44 CONDUIT STREET
LONDON · WIR ODE

200 MADISON AVENUE
NEW YORK, N.Y. 10016

Printed in Great Britain
by The Stellar Press Hatfield
Hertfordshire

CAROLS FOR CHOIRS

NOTE

THESE fifty Christmas carols, mostly for mixed voices, have been chosen and arranged with carol concerts and carol services in mind.

Many of the carols are from traditional sources and include a number of well-loved tunes either newly arranged by the present Editors or in settings by other distinguished musicians both past and present. A little more than half are for unaccompanied singing, the remainder having accompaniments for piano or organ and incorporating varied harmonizations and descants.

Four carols have been written specially for the book by Arnold Cooke, Reginald Jacques, Phyllis Tate, and William Walton; original compositions by Bach, Berlioz, Benjamin Britten, Armstrong Gibbs, John Joubert, and R. Vaughan Williams are also included.

The texts of the now traditional NINE LESSONS are printed as an Appendix, and a leaflet containing the words only of thirteen of the most popular carols, for the use of audiences and congregations, is on sale. The accompaniments to these thirteen carols (see Index) have been arranged for strings, the parts being on hire.

Carols for Choirs is a comprehensive and varied collection, and it is hoped that by using it choirs will be able to perform their Christmas concerts and services without the inconvenience of handling a number of separate leaflets and books.

Note on the NINE LESSONS

The service of Nine Lessons with Carols was first drawn up by Archbishop Benson when Bishop of Truro for use in that Cathedral, and was later simplified and modified for use in King's College Chapel, Cambridge, in 1918 by its then Dean, the Very Reverend Eric Milner-White, to whom also we owe the Bidding Prayer.

Fourteen of the carols in this collection are included on the record *Family Carols* (SCX3562), and ten on the record *More Family Carols* (SCX6179), sung by The Bach Choir, with the Jacques Orchestra, conducted by David Willcocks.
Both records are issued by EMI.

Accompaniments for strings (some with optional keyboard) are available for all the carols listed below. In addition, the following material is available:

ORCHESTRAL ACCOMPANIMENTS

*For 2 fl., 2 ob., 2 cl., 2 bn., 2 hn., 2 tpt., timp., and strings
†For 2 ob., 2 cl., and strings

A great and mighty wonder
And there were shepherds
(*with keyboard continuo*)
As with gladness
Away in a manger
Carol, with Lullaby
*God rest you merry, gentlemen
*Good King Wenceslas
*Hark! the herald angels sing
It came upon the midnight clear
Lute-Book Lullaby
*O come, all ye faithful
*O little town of Bethlehem
Once in royal David's city
Rocking
*See amid the winter's snow
†Shepherds' Farewell
*Sussex Carol (*with keyboard in strings version*)
*The First Nowell
*Unto us is born a Son
We wish you a merry Christmas
While shepherds watched

BRASS ACCOMPANIMENTS

For 3 tpt. and 3 tmb., or 2 hn., 2 tpt., 2 tmb., and opt. tuba and timp.

O come, all ye faithful
O little town of Bethlehem
See amid the winter's snow
The First Nowell
Unto us is born a Son

For 4 tpt., 3 tmb., tuba, timp., and percussion

God rest you merry, gentlemen
Good King Wenceslas
(*with optional organ part*)
Hark! the herald angels sing
O come, all ye faithful
Once in royal David's city
The First Nowell
Unto us is born a Son
While shepherds watched

For 2 tpt., hn., tmb., and tuba

As with gladness
God rest you merry, gentlemen
Good King Wenceslas
Hark! the herald angels sing
O come, all ye faithful
O little town of Bethlehem
See amid the winter's snow
Unto us is born a Son
While shepherds watched

For 2 tpt., hn. (or tpt. 3), tmb., tuba, and percussion

We wish you a merry Christmas

The carols 'God rest you', 'O come, all ye faithful', 'Unto us is born a Son', 'The First Nowell', and 'Hark! the herald angels sing' are published together under the title *Five Christmas Carols*. The carols 'Good King Wenceslas', 'O little town of Bethlehem', and 'See amid the winter's snow' are published together under the title *Three Carol Orchestrations*. Full scores and parts for the orchestrations of these carols are on sale.

INDEX OF TITLES AND FIRST LINES

Where first lines differ from titles the former are shown in italics.

Carols suitable for unaccompanied singing are marked thus *.
Accompaniment for strings is available on hire †.

continued overleaf

INDEX OF TITLES AND FIRST LINES

The words of the following carols make up the congregation/audience words leaflet, published separately:

A GREAT AND MIGHTY WONDER
AS WITH GLADNESS MEN OF OLD
GOD REST YOU MERRY, GENTLEMEN
GOOD KING WENCESLAS
HARK! THE HERALD ANGELS SING
IT CAME UPON THE MIDNIGHT CLEAR
O COME, ALL YE FAITHFUL
O LITTLE TOWN OF BETHLEHEM
ONCE IN ROYAL DAVID'S CITY
SEE AMID THE WINTER'S SNOW
THE FIRST NOWELL
UNTO US IS BORN A SON
WHILE SHEPHERDS WATCHED THEIR FLOCKS

1. A GREAT AND MIGHTY WONDER

Words by St. GERMANUS (634-734)
tr. J. M. NEALE

Old German tune
harmonized by M. PRAETORIUS
(1571-1621)

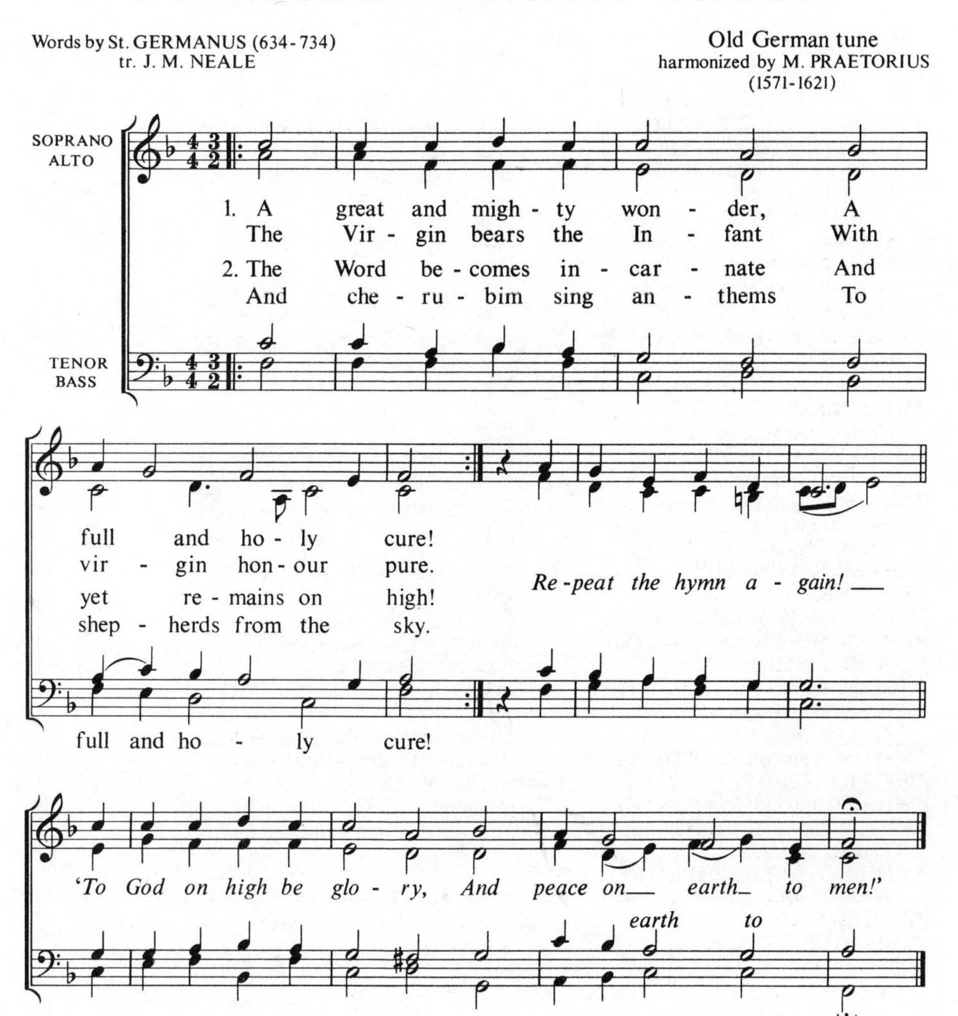
SOPRANO
ALTO
TENOR
BASS
1. A great and migh - ty won - der, A
The Vir - gin bears the In - fant With
2. The Word be - comes in - car - nate And
And che - ru - bim sing an - thems To
full and ho - ly cure!
vir - gin hon - our pure.
yet re - mains on high!
shep - herds from the sky.
Re - peat the hymn a - gain!
full and ho - ly cure!
'To God on high be glo - ry, And peace on earth to men!'
earth to

The barring of this tune is necessarily irregular. But its performance will be found to be easy if it is remembered that the time-value of a crotchet is the same throughout.

3. While thus they sing your monarch,
 Those bright angelic bands,
Rejoice, ye vales and mountains,
 Ye oceans clap your hands.
Repeat the hymn again! etc.

4. Since all he comes to ransom,
 By all be he adored,
The Infant born in Bethl'em
 The Saviour and the Lord.
Repeat the hymn again! etc.

5. And idol forms shall perish,
 And error shall decay,
And Christ shall wield his sceptre,
 Our Lord and God for ay.
Repeat the hymn again! etc.

2. AWAY IN A MANGER

(First tune)

Words anon.

Tune by W. J. KIRKPATRICK (1838-1921)
arranged by DAVID WILLCOCKS

In verse 3 the whole choir may hum whilst a treble soloist sings the words.

2. AWAY IN A MANGER

(Second tune)

Words anon.

Traditional Normandy tune
arranged by REGINALD JACQUES

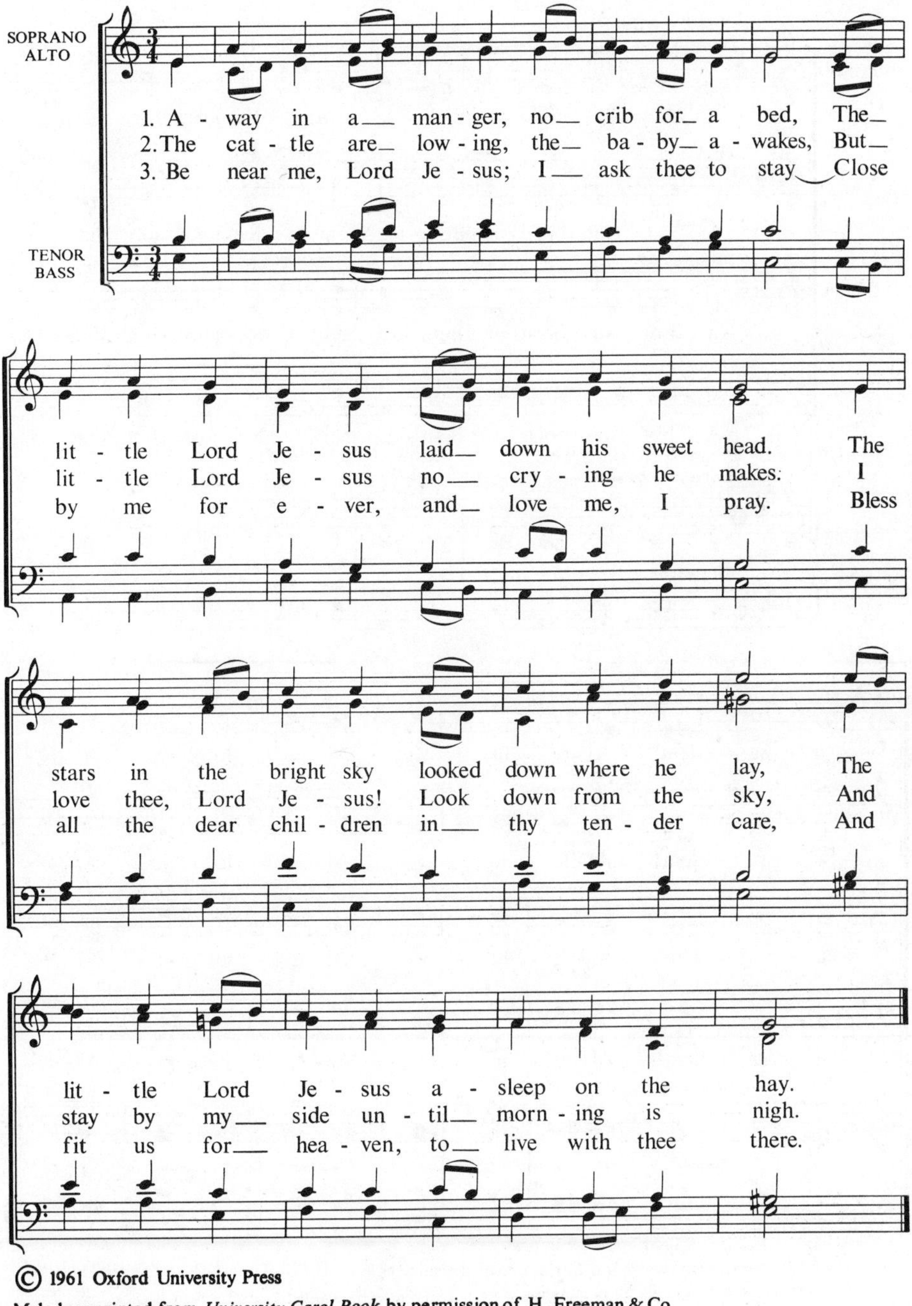
SOPRANO
ALTO
1. A - way in a__ man - ger, no__ crib for_ a bed, The_
2. The cat - tle are_ low - ing, the_ ba - by_ a - wakes, But_
3. Be near me, Lord Je - sus; I__ ask thee to stay Close
TENOR
BASS
lit - tle Lord Je - sus laid_ down his sweet head. The
lit - tle Lord Je - sus no__ cry - ing he makes. I
by me for e - ver, and_ love me, I pray. Bless
stars in the bright sky looked down where he lay, The
love thee, Lord Je - sus! Look down from the sky, And
all the dear chil - dren in__ thy ten - der care, And
lit - tle Lord Je - sus a - sleep on the hay.
stay by my__ side un - til__ morn - ing is nigh.
fit us for__ hea - ven, to__ live with thee there.

Melody reprinted from *University Carol Book* by permission of H. Freeman & Co.

To my father

3. A BOY WAS BORN

16th century
German words
Tr. PERCY DEARMER

BENJAMIN BRITTEN

This is the theme from the Choral Variations of the same title. (O.U.P.) The words are reprinted from *The Oxford Book of Carols* by permission.

p
(𝄐) più f
-lu - - ya. He let him-self a ser-vant be, That all man-
mf
mf (il basso marcato)
-kind he might set free: Al-le-lu - - ya, Al-le-
f

ff
sf
f marcato
-lu - ya, Al - le - lu - ya, Al - le - lu - - ya. Then

mf
dim.
praise the Word of God who came To dwell with - in a

sempre più p
p
pp
hu - man frame: Al - le - lu - ya, Al - le - lu - ya, Al - le -
Rall.
- lu - ya, Al - le - lu - ya, Al - le - lu - - - - ya.

4. AS WITH GLADNESS MEN OF OLD

Words by
W. CHATTERTON DIX

Abridged from a chorale, *Treuer Heiland*,
by C. KOCHER, 1786-1872
arranged by DAVID WILLCOCKS

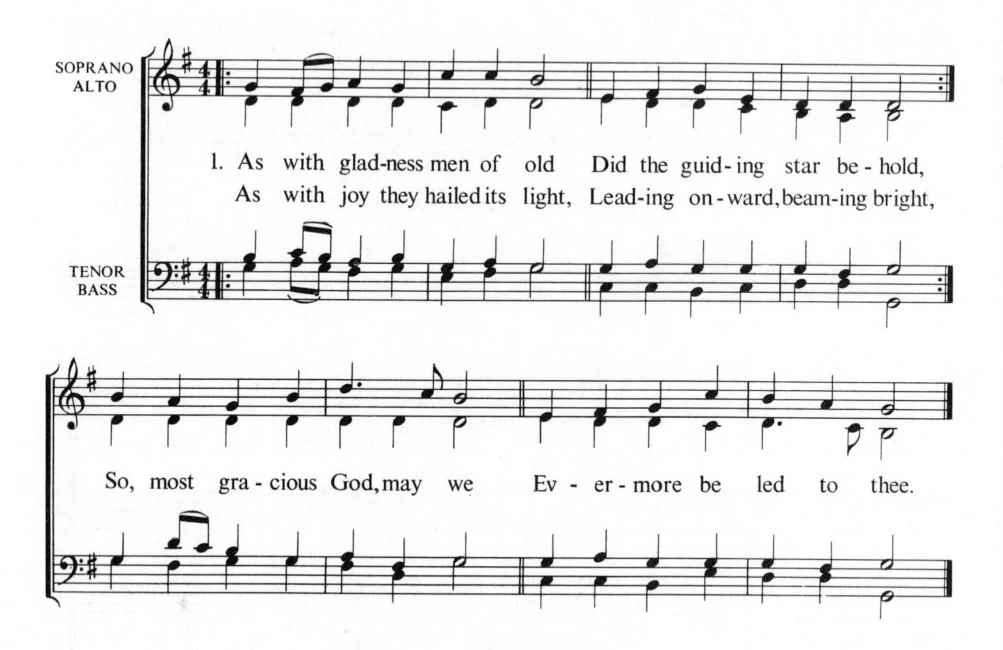

SOPRANO
ALTO
TENOR
BASS
1. As with glad-ness men of old Did the guid-ing star be-hold,
As with joy they hailed its light, Lead-ing on-ward, beam-ing bright,
So, most gra-cious God, may we Ev-er-more be led to thee.

2. As with joyful steps they sped,
To that lowly manger-bed,
There to bend the knee before
Him whom heaven and earth adore,
So may we with willing feet
Ever seek thy mercy-seat.

3. As they offered gifts most rare
At that manger rude and bare,
So may we with holy joy,
Pure, and free from sin's alloy,
All our costliest treasures bring,
Christ, to thee our heavenly King.

4. Holy Jesu, every day
Keep us in the narrow way;
And, when earthly things are past,
Bring our ransomed souls at last
Where they need no star to guide,
Where no clouds thy glory hide.

The harmonies used for verses 1-4 are from *The English Hymnal*. It is suggested that verse 4 is sung by the choir only, unaccompanied.

Choir I and Congregation
Choir II and Organ or Piano
5. In the heav'n-ly coun-try bright Need they no cre - a - ted light;
5. In the heav'n-ly coun-try bright_ Need they no_ cre - a - ted light;
Thou its_ light, its joy, its crown, Thou its sun which goes not down:
Thou its light, its joy, its_ crown,_ Thou its sun which goes not down:
There for e - ver may we sing Al - le - lu - yas to our King.
There for_ e - ver sing Al-le-lu - yas_ to our King.
There for e - ver_ sing___ Al - le - lu - yas_ to our King.

5. AND THERE WERE SHEPHERDS

J.S. BACH
(from *Christmas Oratorio*)
edited by DAVID WILLCOCKS

The words of the recitative are from Luke ii vv. 8-11

From bar 2 the accompaniment is as scored by Bach for strings (Bach's figures have been included so that the bass may be fully realised).

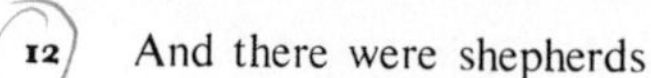

CHORALE
SOPRANO
(f)
Break forth, O beauteous heav'nly light, And ush-er in the morn-ing; Ye
ALTO
(f)
Break forth, O beauteous heav'nly light, And ush-er_ in the morn-ing; Ye
TENOR
(f)
Break forth,_ O beauteous heav'nly light, And ush-er_ in the morn-ing; Ye
BASS
(f)
Break forth, O beauteous heav'nly light, And ush-er_ in_ the_ morn-ing; Ye_
PIANO or ORGAN
(f)

(mp)
shep-herds, shrink not with af-fright, But hear the an-gel's warn - ing. This
shep-herds, shrink not with_ af-fright, But hear the_ an-gel's warn - ing. This
shep - herds, shrink not with af-fright, But_ hear_ the_ an-gel's warn - ing. This
shep-herds, shrink not_ with af-fright, But hear_ the_ an-gel's warn - ing. This
(mp)

(cresc.)
(ff)
child, now weak in in - fan - cy, Our con - fi - dence and joy shall be, The
child, now weak in in - fan - cy, Our_ con - fi - dence and_ joy_ shall be, The
child, now weak in in - fan - cy, Our_ con - fi - dence and joy shall be, The
child, now weak in in - fan - cy, Our_ con - fi - dence and joy shall be, The
(p)
pow'r of Sa - tan break - ing, Our peace e - ter - nal_ mak - ing.
pow'r of Sa - tan_ break - ing, Our_ peace e - ter - nal mak - ing.
pow'r of Sa - tan break - ing, Our peace e - ter - nal mak - ing.
pow'r of_ Sa - tan_ break - ing, Our peace e - ter - nal mak - ing.

6. A VIRGIN MOST PURE

English traditional carol
arranged by CHARLES WOOD

SOPRANO
ALTO
TENOR
BASS
1. A vir - gin most pure, as the pro- phets do tell, Hath
2. In Beth- le - hem Jew- ry a ci - ty there was, Where
brought forth a ba - by, as it hath be - fell; To be our Re -
Jo - seph and Ma - ry to - geth - er did pass, And there to be
- deem - er from death, hell, and sin, Which A - dam's trans -
tax - ed with ma - ny one mo, For Cae - sar com -
- gres - sion had wrap-ped us in.
- mand - ed the same should be so.
Aye, and there - fore be

* In verse 4 these slurred notes must be split

Reprinted from *The Cowley Carol Book* by permission

mer - ry; Re - joice, and be you mer - ry; Set_ sor - row a -
- side; Christ Je - sus our Sa - viour was_ born_ at this_ tide.

3. But when they had enter'd the city so fair,
A number of people so mighty was there,
That Joseph and Mary, whose substance was small,
Could find in the inn there no lodging at all.
Aye, and therefore, etc.

4. Then they were constrain'd in a stable to lie,
Where horses and asses they us'd for to tie;
Their lodging so simple they took it no scorn,
But against the next morning our Saviour was born.
Aye, and therefore, etc.

5. The King of all kings to this world being brought,
Small store of fine linen to wrap him was sought;
And when she had swaddled her young son so sweet,
Within an ox-manger she laid him to sleep.
Aye, and therefore, etc.

6. Then God sent an angel from heaven so high,
To certain poor shepherds in fields where they lie,
And bade them no longer in sorrow to stay,
Because that our Saviour was born on this day.
Aye, and therefore, etc.

7. Then presently after the shepherds did spy
A number of angels that stood in the sky;
They joyfully talkèd and sweetly did sing,
'To God be all glory our heavenly King.'
Aye, and therefore, etc.

7. ANGELS, FROM THE REALMS OF GLORY

Words by J. MONTGOMERY

Old French tune arranged by REGINALD JACQUES

SOPRANO I
SOPRANO II
1. An-gels, from the realms of glo - ry, Wing your flight o'er all the earth;
2. Shep-herds in the field a - bi-ding, Watch-ing o'er your flocks by night,
ALTO
SOPRANO
ALTO
Ye who sang cre - a - tion's sto-ry Now pro-claim Mes - si - ah's birth:
God with man is now re - si-ding; Yon-der shines the in - fant light:
TENOR
SOPRANO
ALTO
Glo - ri - a
Glo - ri - a
in ex - cel - sis De - o,
TENOR
BASS
Glo - ri - a

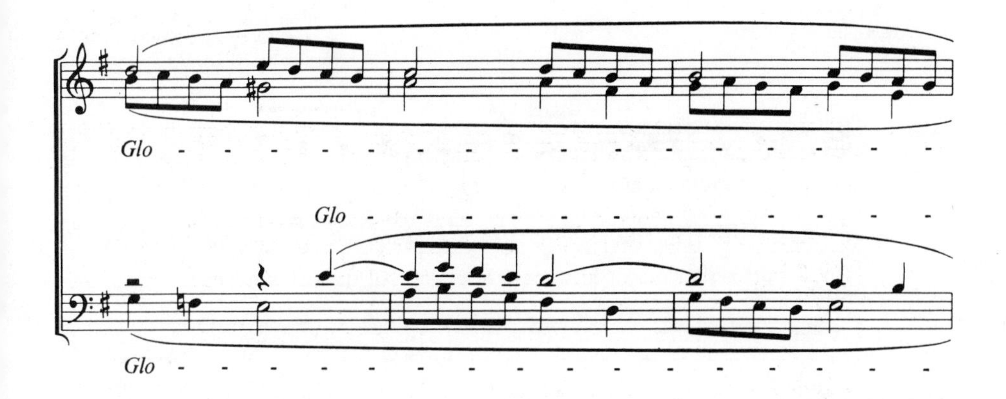
Glo
Glo
Glo

ri - a
in ex - cel - sis De - - - - - o.
ri - a
ri - a

Montgomery's original words for the refrain were *Come and worship, Worship Christ the new-born King.*

3. Sages, leave your contemplations;
   Brighter visions beam afar;
   Seek the great desire of nations;
   Ye have seen his natal star:
   Gloria in excelsis Deo.

4. Saints before the altar bending,
   Watching long in hope and fear,
   Suddenly the Lord, descending,
   In his temple shall appear:
   Gloria in excelsis Deo.

5. Though an infant now we view him,
   He shall fill his Father's throne,
   Gather all the nations to him;
   Every knee shall then bow down:
   Gloria in excelsis Deo.

8. A CHRISTMAS CAROL

Words by
CLEMENT F. ROGERS

Hungarian traditional tune
arranged by ZOLTAN KODALY

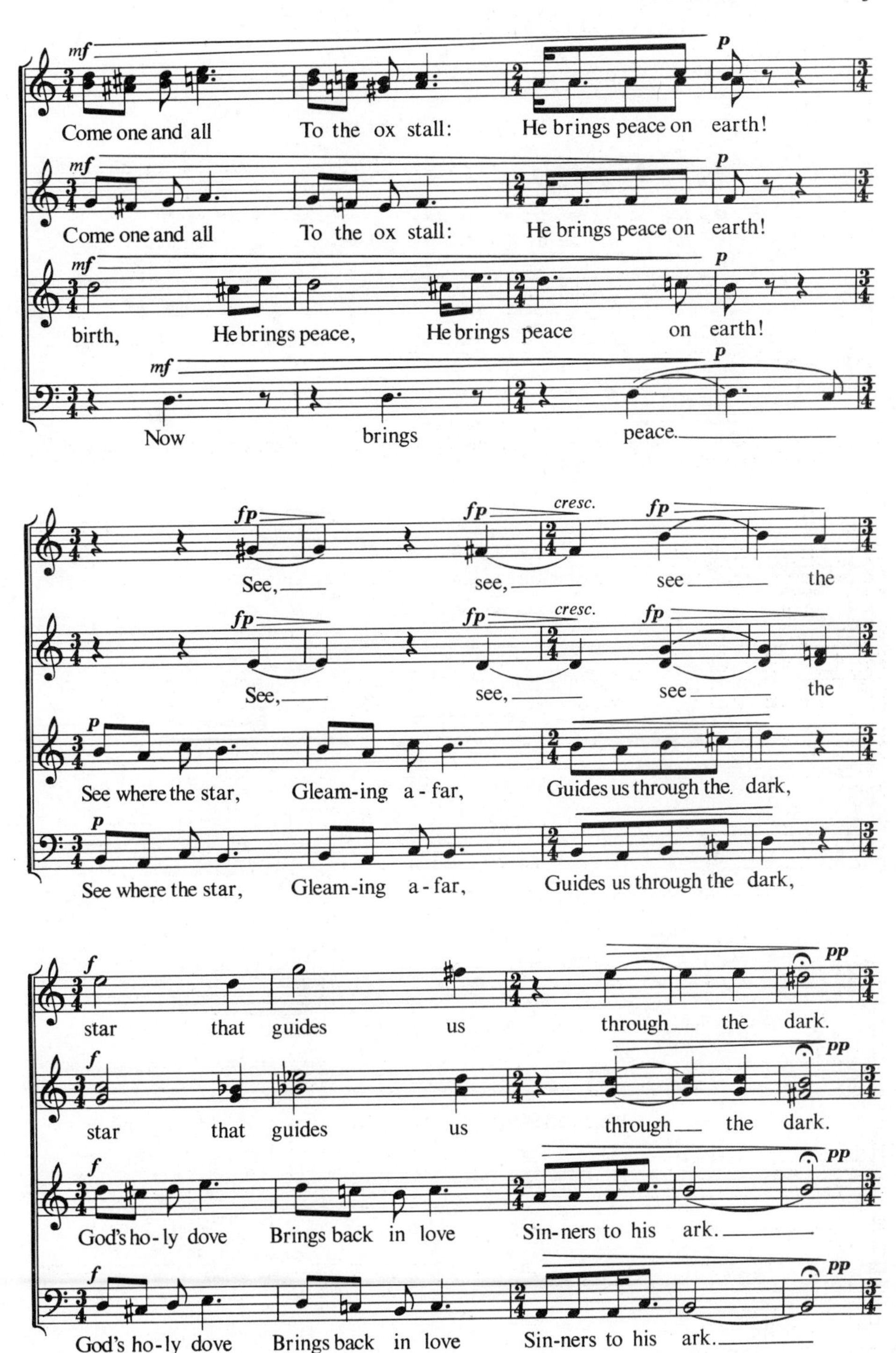
Come one and all To the ox stall: He brings peace on earth!
Come one and all To the ox stall: He brings peace on earth!
birth, He brings peace, He brings peace on earth!
Now brings peace.
See, see, see the
See, see, see the
See where the star, Gleam-ing a - far, Guides us through the dark,
See where the star, Gleam-ing a - far, Guides us through the dark,
star that guides us through the dark.
star that guides us through the dark.
God's ho-ly dove Brings back in love Sin-ners to his ark.
God's ho-ly dove Brings back in love Sin-ners to his ark.

p
Tell the sto- ry Of his glo-ry, Christ by all a - dored.
p
Tell the sto- ry Of his glo-ry, Christ by all a - dored.
p
Tell the sto - ry Of his glo - ry, Christ by all a - dored.
p
Tell the sto - ry Of his glo - ry, Christ by all a - dored.
cresc.
f
Songs up-rais-ing, Praise him, praise him, All men praise the Lord.
f
Songs up-rais-ing, Praise him, praise him, All men praise the Lord.
f
Songs up-rais-ing, Praise him, praise him, All men praise the Lord.
f
Songs up-rais-ing, Praise him, praise him, All men praise the Lord.
pp
Babe all ho-ly, Whom all low-ly Ox and ass a - dore,
pp
Babe all ho - ly, Whom all low-ly Ox and ass a -
pp
Babe all ho-ly whom ox and ass a - dore,
pp
Babe all ho- ly whom all low-ly Ox and ass a - dore,

Bless our cat - tle, Bless our har - vest, Bless each house and
- dore, Bless our cat - tle, Bless our har - vest,
Bless our cat - tle, Bless our har - vest,
Bless our cat - tle, Bless our har - vest, Bless each house and
p cresc.
store. Je - su, hear us, Christ, be
Bless each house and store. Je - su, hear us, Christ, be
Bless each house and store. Je - su, hear us, Christ, be
store. Je - su, hear us, Christ, be near us,
f
near us, Make us ho - ly, With joy - ful praise
near us, Make us ho - ly, With joy - ful praise
near us, Make us ho - ly, With joy - ful praise
Make us ho - ly all, With joy - ful praise

Fill all our days, Hear us when we call.
Fill all our days, Hear us when we call.
Fill all our days, Hear us when we call.
Fill all our days, Hear us when we call.

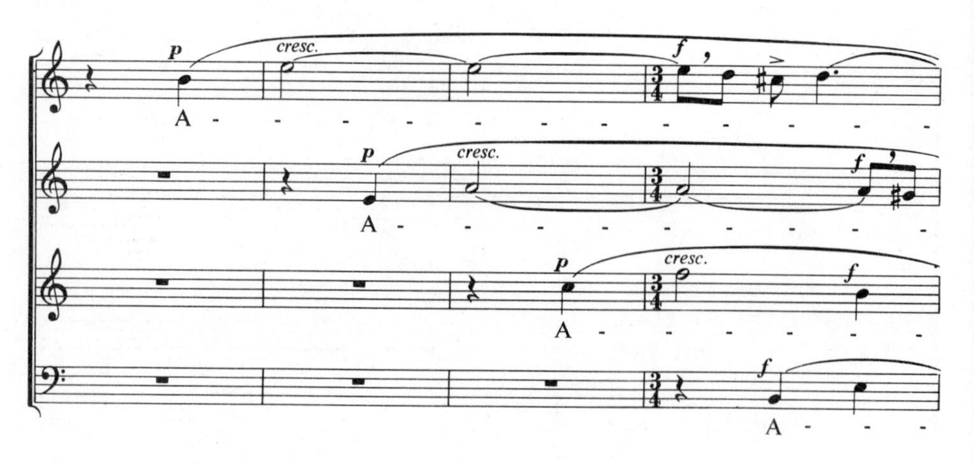
p
cresc.
f
A
A
A
A

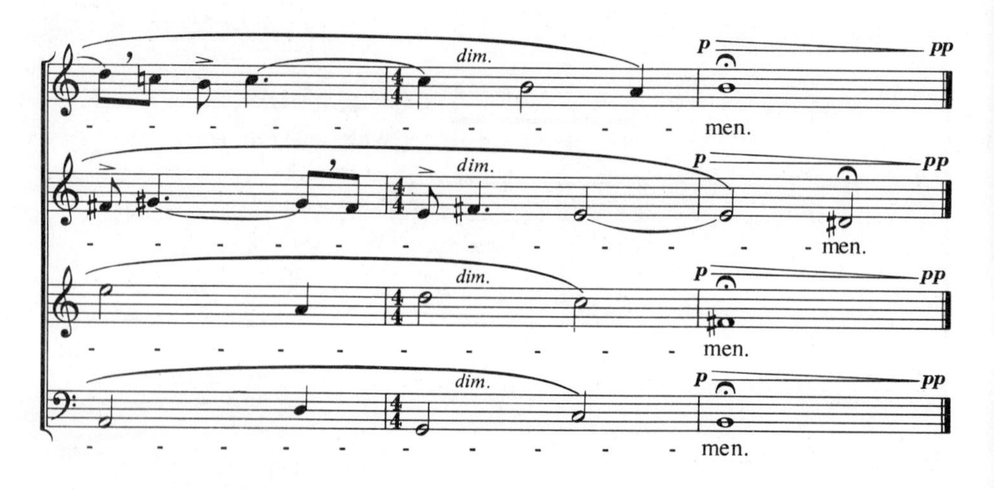
dim.
p
pp
men.
men.
men.
men.

9. BLESSED BE THAT MAID MARY

Words by
G. R. WOODWARD

English traditional tune
arranged by DAVID WILLCOCKS

Words reprinted from *The Cowley Carol Book* by permission

pp sempre
CHOIR I
2. In a man-ger of an ass Je-su lay and lull-ed was;
pp sempre
pp sempre
CHOIR II
Ah
pp sempre
Born to die up-on the tree
Pro pec-can-te ho-mi-ne.
Ah
E-ya! Je-sus ho-di-e Na-tus est de vir-gi-ne.
Ah
Ah
Ah

SOPRANO I
SOPRANO II
ALTO
P legato
3. Sweet and bliss-ful was the song Chant-ed of the an-gel throng,
"Peace on earth", Al - le - lu - ya.
In ex - cel - sis glo - ri - a.
In ex - cel - sis glo-ri-a. E - ya!
In ex - cel - sis glo - ri - a.
E - ya! Je - sus ho - di - e Na - tus est de vir - gi - ne.
Je - sus ho - di - e Na - tus est de vir - gi - ne, de vir - gi - ne.
E - ya! Je - sus ho - di - e Na - tus, na - tus est de vir - gi - ne.
TENOR
BASS I
BASS II
mf
4. Fare three kings from far - off land, In-cense, gold and myrrh in hand;
In Beth-lem the Babe they see, Stel - le duc - ti lu - mi - ne.
In Beth - lem the Babe they see, Stel - le duc - ti lu-mi-ne.
In Beth - lem the Babe they see, Stel - le duc - ti lu - mi - ne.
f
E - ya! Je - sus ho - di - e Na - tus est de vir - gi - ne.
E - ya! Je-sus ho- di - e Na - tus est de vir - gi - ne.
E - ya! Je - sus Na-tus est de vir - gi-ne.

(to next page)

5. Make we mer - ry on this fest, In quo Christ - us
5. Make we mer - ry on this fest, Christ-us
CHOIR I
5. Make we mer - ry on this fest, In quo Christ - us
5. Make we mer - ry on this fest, Christ-us
CHOIR II
5. Make we mer - ry on this fest, In quo Christ-us

na - tus est;
On this child I pray you call,
na - tus est;
na - tus est;
na - tus est; On this child I pray you call,

ff
To— as - soil and save us— all.—— E - ya! Je - sus
ff
To— as - soil— and save, and save us all.

ho - di - e—— Na - tus est de vir - gi - ne.——
E - ya! Je - sus Na - tus est de vir - gi - ne.
ff
ff
Na - tus— est de vir - - gi - ne.
E - ya! Je - sus
E - ya! Je - sus Na - tus est de vir - gi-ne.
ff
ff
E - ya! Je - sus Na - tus— est de vir - - gi - ne.

10. DING DONG! MERRILY ON HIGH

Words by
G. R. WOODWARD

16th c. French tune
harmonized by CHARLES WOOD

SOPRANO
ALTO
TENOR
BASS
1. Ding dong! mer-ri - ly on high in heav'n the bells are ring - ing:
Ding dong! ve-ri - ly the sky is riv'n with an - gel sing - ing.
2. E'en so here be-low, be - low, let stee - ple bells be swung-en,
And i - o, i - o, i - o, by priest and peo - ple sung - en.
3. Pray you, du - ti - ful - ly prime your mat - in chime, ye ring - ers;
May you beau-ti - ful - ly rime your eve -time song, ye sing - ers.
Glo - ri - a, Ho - san - na in ex - cel - sis!

i-o pronounced *ee-o*

Reprinted from *The Cambridge Carol Book* by permission

11. GOD REST YOU MERRY, GENTLEMEN

English traditional carol
arranged by DAVID WILLCOCKS

* If preferred, the refrain may always be sung in unison (with organ accompaniment)

Unison voices

3. The shepherds at those tidings
Rejoicèd much in mind,
And left their flocks a-feeding,
In tempest, storm and wind,
And went to Bethlehem straightway
This blessèd babe to find:
O tidings of comfort and joy.

Unaccompanied voices

4. But when to Bethlehem they came,
Whereat this infant lay,
They found him in a manger,
Where oxen feed on hay;
His mother Mary kneeling,
Unto the Lord did pray:
O tidings of comfort and joy.

SOPRANOS I II
Ah
Ah
ALTOS
TENORS and BASSES
5. Now to the Lord sing prais - es, All you with- in this place, And
Sw.
ORGAN
Gt.
Ped.

Ah
Ah
Ah
with true love and bro-ther-hood Each o-ther now em- brace; This ho- ly tide of

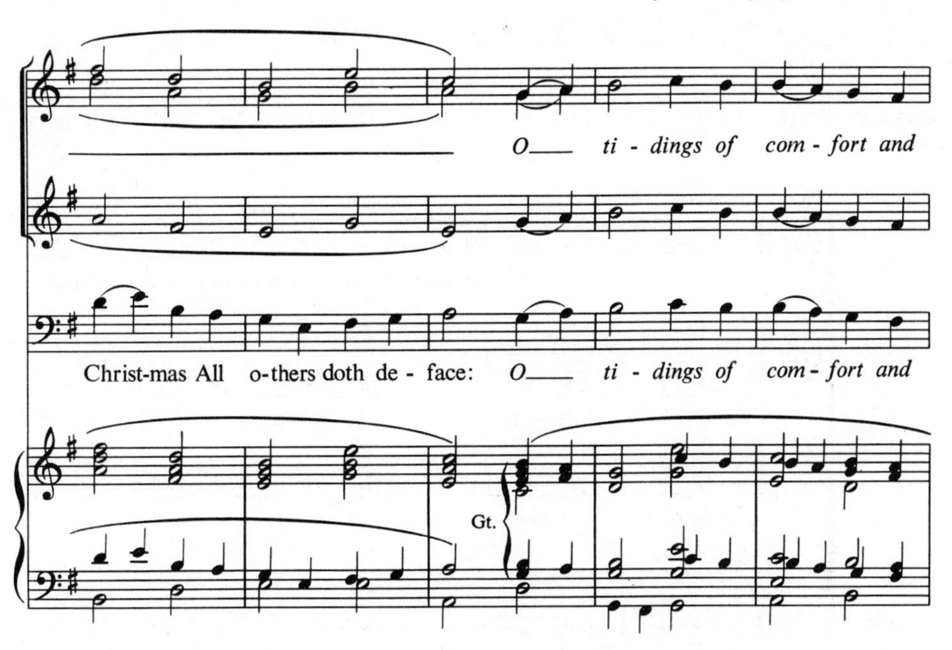
O— ti - dings of com - fort and
Christ-mas All o-thers doth de - face: O— ti - dings of com - fort and
Gt.

joy, com-fort and joy, O— ti - dings of com - fort and joy.
joy, com-fort and joy, O— ti - dings of com - fort and joy.

12. ZITHER CAROL

Words by
MALCOLM SARGENT

Czech folk tune
arranged by MALCOLM SARGENT

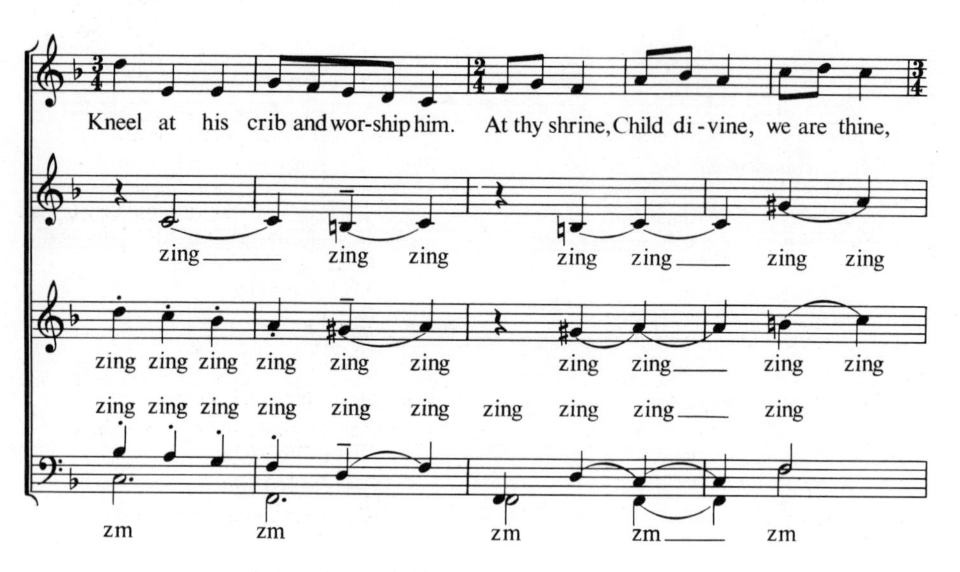

* *zing* pronounced *tzing*
zm pronounced *tzoomm*

All slurred notes to be sung *legato* and with *glissando*

2. *p* On that day-far away-Jesus lay,
Angels were watching round his head.
Holy Child-Mother mild-undefiled,
cresc. We sing thy praise.
f "*Hallelujah*" *etc.*
Our hearts we raise.

3. *mf* Shepherds came-at the fame-of thy name,
Angels their guide to Bethlehem.
In that place-saw thy face-filled with grace,
Stood at thy door.
f "*Hallelujah*" *etc.*
Love evermore.

4. *mf* Wise men too-haste to do-homage new,
Gold, myrrh and frankincense they bring.
As 'twas said-starlight led-to thy bed,
p Bending their knee.
f "*Hallelujah*" *etc.*
Worshipping thee.

5. *pp* Oh, that we-all might be-good as he,
Spotless, with God in Unity.
cresc. Saviour dear-ever near-with us here
Since life began.
f "*Hallelujah*" *etc.*
Godhead made man.

6. *f* Cherubim-Seraphim-worship him,
Sun, moon and stars proclaim his power.
Everyday-on our way-we shall say
ff Hallelujah.
ff "*Hallelujah*" *etc.*
Hallelujah.

13. GOOD KING WENCESLAS

Words by J. M. NEALE

Tune from *Piae Cantiones*
arranged by REGINALD JACQUES

ORGAN
or
PIANO
SOPRANO
ALTO
(ORGAN
or
PIANO)
TENOR
BASS
f
1. Good King Wen-ces-las look'd out On the Feast of Ste-phen,
When the snow lay round a-bout, Deep, and crisp, and e-ven:
Bright-ly shone the moon that night, Though the frost was cru-el,
When a poor man came in sight, Ga-th'ring win-ter fu-el.

Note: The harmonies used for verse 1 and the second part of verse 3 are by Sir John Stainer (1840-1901)

† small notes for piano

TENORS and BASSES
mf
3. 'Bring me flesh, and bring me wine, Bring me pine-logs hi - ther:
ORGAN or PIANO
mf
Thou and I will see him dine, When we bear them thi - ther.'
SOPRANO ALTO
f
(ORGAN or PIANO)
Page and mon-arch, forth they went, Forth they went to - ge - ther;
TENOR BASS
f
Through the rude wind's wild la - ment And the bit - ter wea - - ther.

SOPRANOS and ALTOS
mp
4. 'Sire, the night is darker now, And the wind blows stronger;
ORGAN or PIANO
mp
Fails my heart, I know not how; I can go no longer.'
TENORS and BASSES
f
'Mark my foot-steps, good my page; Tread thou in them boldly:
ORGAN or PIANO
f
Thou shalt find the winter's rage Freeze thy blood less coldly.'

DESCANT (SOPRANOS)
ALL OTHER VOICES
ORGAN or PIANO
f
5. In his ma - ster's steps he trod, Where the snow lay din - ted; Heat was in the ve - ry sod Which the Saint had prin - ted.
There-fore, Chris-tian men, be sure, Wealth or rank pos - sess - ing,
Ye who now will bless the poor, Shall your - selves find bless - - - ing.
ff

14. HARK! THE HERALD ANGELS SING

Words by C. WESLEY,
T. WHITEFIELD, M. MADAN
and others

MENDELSSOHN
Descant and organ part by
DAVID WILLCOCKS

SOPRANO
ALTO

(ORGAN)

TENOR
BASS

f 1. Hark! the he - rald an - gels sing_ Glo - ry to the new - born King;
mf 2. Christ, by high - est heav'n a - dored, Christ, the e - ver - last - ing Lord,

Peace on earth and mer - cy mild,_ God and sin - ners re - con - ciled:
Late in time be - hold him come_ Off - spring of a vir - gin's womb:

Joy - ful all ye na - tions rise,_ Join the tri - umph of the skies,_
Veiled in flesh the God - head see,_ Hail th'in - car - nate De - i - ty!_

With th'an - gel - ic host pro - claim, Christ is _ born in Beth - le hem.
Pleased as man with man to dwell, Je - sus, _ our Em - ma - nu - el.

Unison

Org.

f Hark! the he - rald an - gels sing Glo - ry _ to the new - born King.

Org. ped.

Melody, and harmony for vv. 1 and 2, adapted by W. H. Cummings (1831-1915) from a chorus by Mendelssohn.
Verses 1 and 2 may be sung by unison voices and organ if desired. *Deity* pronounced *Dee-ity*

DESCANT (SOPRANOS)
ALL OTHER VOICES
ORGAN
f 3. Hail the heav'n-born Prince of Peace! Hail the Sun of
Right-eous-ness! Light and life to all he brings, Risen with heal-ing
in his wings; Mild he lays his glo-ry by, Born that man no
f

more may_ die,___ Born to raise the_ sons of earth,
ff
Born to give them se - cond birth. Hark! the he - rald
ff
ff
an - gels_ sing___ Glo - ry___ to___ the___ new - born King.

15. IN DULCI JUBILO

Edited and adapted by REGINALD JACQUES

Old German tune
arranged by R. L. PEARSALL

The original melody employed, as a *Cantus firmus*, in the following composition, is to be found in an old German book published in the year 1570,—which, from its title and contents, appears to have contained the ritual of the Protestant Congregations of Zweibrueken and Neuburg. Even there it is called "a very ancient song *(uraltes Lied)* for Christmas-eve;" so that there can be no doubt that it is one of those old Roman Catholic melodies that Luther, on account of their beauty, retained in the Protestant Service. It was formerly sung in the processions that took place on Christmas-eve, and is so still in those remote parts of Germany where people yet retain old customs. The words are rather remarkable, being written half in Latin and half in the upper German dialect. I have translated them to fit the music, and endeavoured to preserve, as much as I could, the simplicity of the original. Of the melody there can be but one opinion; namely, that which in spite of religious animosity, secured it the approbation of the Protestant reformers, and that of the German people during many centuries. The music in the following passages was written for the Choral Society at Carlsruhe, and was performed there in the Autumn of 1834.
Willsbridge, Gloucestershire, 31st of January, 1837. R. L. P.

VERSE 1: CHOIR I
VERSE 2: CHOIR II

Moderato

SOPRANO
p *dim.*
1. In dul - ci ju - bi - lo Let us our hom - age
2. O Je - su par - vu - le! I yearn for thee al-

ALTO
p *dim.*
1. In dul - ci ju - bi - lo Let us our hom - age
2. O Je - su par - vu - le! I yearn for thee al-

TENOR
p *dim.*
1. In dul - ci ju - bi - lo Let us our hom - age
2. O Je - su par - vu - le! I yearn for thee al-

BASS
p *dim.*
1. In dul - ci ju - bi - lo Let us our hom - age
2. O Je - su par - vu - le! I yearn for thee al-

Moderato
(For practice only)
p *dim.*

EDITOR'S NOTE

Pearsall wrote the following footnote in his original: 'The time of this melody should not be taken very slow. It must be borne in mind that the Semibreve and Minim were two of the shortest notes employed by Ancient Composers.'
Pearsall's translation of the second line of verse 2 was 'My heart is sore for thee!'
The expression marks are Pearsall's.

p
shew; Our heart's joy re - cli - - neth
-way! Hear me, I be - seech thee,
shew; Our heart's joy re - cli - - neth
-way! Hear me, I be - seech thee,
shew; Our heart's joy re - cli - - neth
-way! Hear me, I be - seech thee,
shew; Our heart's joy re - cli - - neth
-way! Hear me, I be - seech thee,
LOOK
catch
cresc.
In præ - se - pi - o And like a bright star
O Puer op - ti - me! My prayer let it
In præ - se - pi - o And like a bright star
O Puer op - ti - me! My prayer let it
In præ - se - pi - o And like a bright star
O Puer op - ti - me! My prayer let it
In præ - se - pi - o And like a bright star
O Puer op - ti - me! My prayer let it

dim.
shi - neth, Ma - tris in gre - mi - o.
reach thee, O Prin - ceps glo - ri - æ!
dim.
shi - neth, Ma - tris in gre - mi - o.
reach thee, O Prin - ceps glo - ri - æ!
dim.
shi - neth, Ma - tris in gre - mi - o.
reach thee, O Prin - ceps glo - ri - æ!
dim.
shi - neth, Ma - tris in gre - mi - o.
reach thee, O Prin - ceps glo - ri - æ!
dim.
CHOIRS I and II
f
dim.
D.C. for Verse 2
Al - pha es et O, Al - pha es et O.
Tra - he me post te! tra - he me post te!
f
dim.
Al - pha es et O, Al - pha es et O.
Tra - he me post te! tra - he me post te!
f
dim.
Al - pha es et O, Al - pha es et O.
Tra - he me post te! tra - he me post te!
f
dim.
Al - pha es et O, Al - pha es et O.
Tra - he me post te! tra - he me post te!
f
dim.
D.C. for Verse 2

*or a few voices

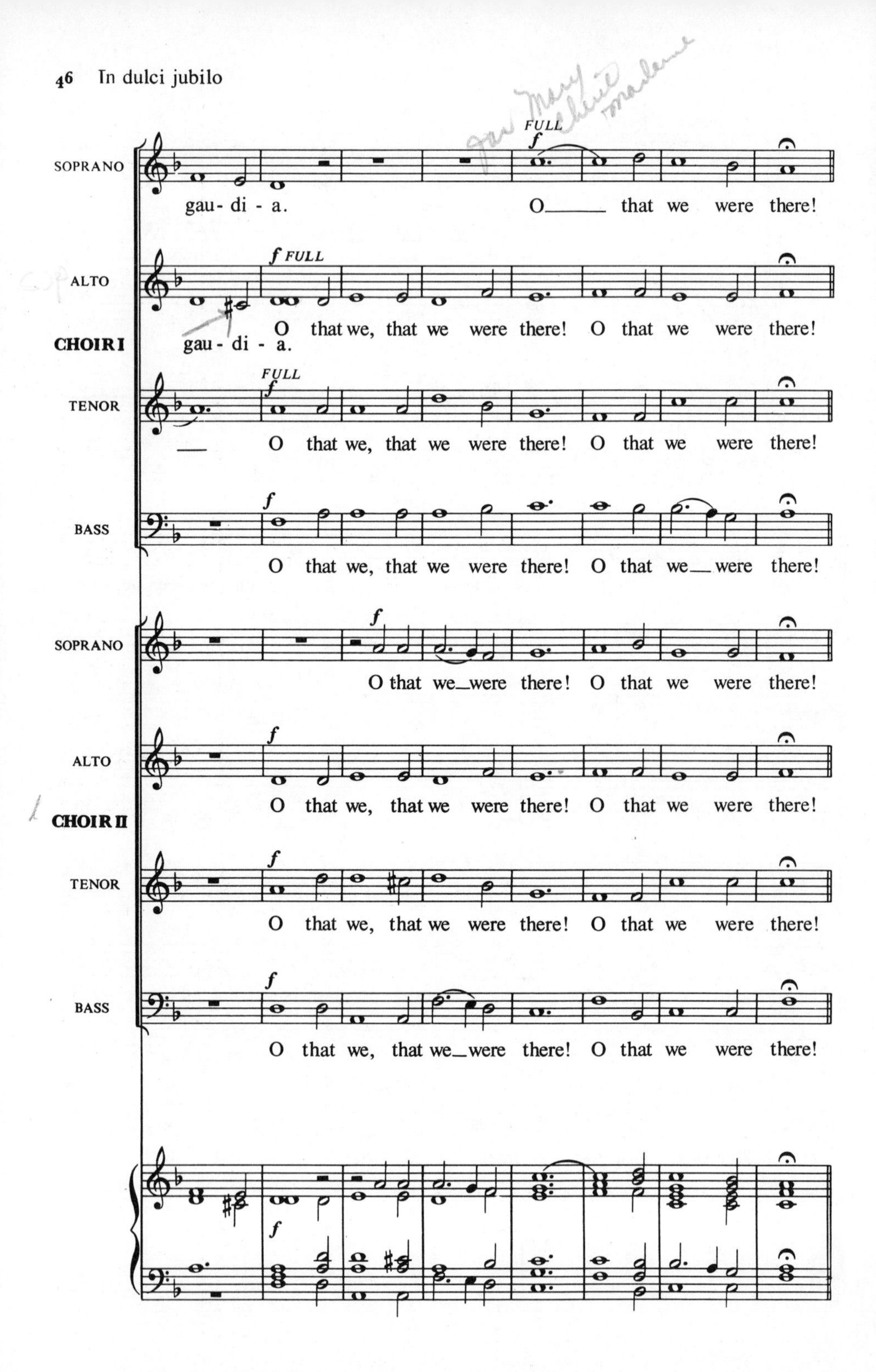
SOPRANO
ALTO
CHOIR I
TENOR
BASS
FULL
f FULL
gau - di - a.
O that we were there!
O that we, that we were there! O that we were there!
O that we, that we were there! O that we were there!
O that we, that we were there! O that we were there!
SOPRANO
ALTO
CHOIR II
TENOR
BASS
f
O that we were there! O that we were there!
O that we, that we were there! O that we were there!
O that we, that we were there! O that we were there!
O that we, that we were there! O that we were there!

f
4. U - bi sunt gau-di-a, where, If that they be not there?
f
4. U - bi sunt gau - di - a, If that they be not there?
f
4. U - bi sunt gau-di- a, where, If that they be not there?
f
4. U - bi, u - bi sunt gau-di-a, where, If not there?
f
4. U - bi sunt gau - di - a, where, If that they be not there?
f
4. U - bi sunt gau - di - a, If that they be not there?
f
4. U - bi sunt gau-di-a, where, If that they be not there?
f
4. U - bi, u - bi sunt gau-di- a, where, If not there?
f

*or a few voices

bells are ring - ing In Re - gis cu - ri - a:
FULL
f
- ing In Re - - - - gis cu - ri - a: O that we were
FULL
f
In Re - gis cu - ri - a: O that we were
FULL
f
ring - - - - ing In Re - gis cu - - ri - a: O that
FULL
f
bells are ring - ing In Re - gis cu - ri - a: O that we were there,
FULL
f
In Re - gis cu - ri - a: O that we were
FULL
f
ells are ring - ing In cu - ri - a: O that we were
FULL
f
ring - ing there In Re - gis cu - ri - a: O that
f

CHOIRS I and II
SOPRANOS (FULL)
f
O that we were there. There are an - -
ALTOS
there, were there, were there. There are
TENORS
there, O that we were there. There are an - gels
1st. BASSES
we were there. There are an - gels sing - - ing,
2nd. BASSES
we were there. There are an - gels sing - - - - -
- - gels sing - ing, There the bells are ring - - - -
an - gels sing - ing, There the bells are ring - - - -
sing - ing, There the bells are ring - ing, the bells are
There the bells are ring - - ing, the bells are ring - - - ing In
- - - - - - - - - ing, the bells are ring - - - ing In

dim.
f
-ing In Re - gis cu - - - ri - a: O that
-ing In Re - gis cu - - - ri - a: O that
ring - ing In Re - - - - - gis cu - ri - a: O that
Re - gis cu - - - - - ri - a: O that
Re - gis ri - a: O that
we were there, O that we were there!
we were there, O that we were there!
we were there, O that we were there!
we were there, O that we were there!
we were there, O that we were there!

16. INFANT HOLY, INFANT LOWLY

Tr. EDITH M. REED

Polish carol
arranged by DAVID WILLCOCKS

Simply

pp legato

SOPRANO

1. In-fant ho-ly, In-fant low-ly, For his bed a cat-tle stall;
2. Flocks were sleep-ing, Shep-herds keep-ing Vi-gil till the morn-ing new;

ALTO

1. In-fant ho-ly,_ In-fant low-ly,_ For his bed a cat-tle stall;_
2. Flocks were sleep-ing, Shep-herds keep-ing Vi-gil till the morn-ing new;_

TENOR

1. In-fant ho-ly,_ In-fant low-ly,_ For his bed a cat-tle stall;_
2. Flocks were sleep-ing, Shep-herds keep-ing Vi-gil till the morn-ing new;_

BASS

1. In-fant ho-ly, In-fant low-ly, For his bed a cat-tle stall;_
2. Flocks were sleep-ing, Shep-herds keep-ing Vi-gil till the morn-ing new;_

(*for practice only*) *pp*

Soprano: Ox-en low-ing, Lit-tle know-ing Christ the Babe is Lord of all.
Saw the glo-ry, Heard the sto-ry, Ti-dings of a gos-pel true.

poco

Alto: Ox-en low-ing,_ Lit-tle know-ing_ Christ the Babe is Lord of all.
Saw the glo-ry,_ Heard the sto-ry,_ Ti-dings of a gos-pel true.

poco *p cresc.*

Tenor: Ox-en low-ing, Lit-tle know-ing Christ the Babe is Lord of all. Swift are
Saw the glo-ry, Heard the sto-ry, Ti-dings of a gos-pel true. Thus re-

poco

Bass: Ox-en low-ing, Lit-tle know-ing Christ the Babe is Lord of all.
Saw the glo-ry, Heard the sto-ry, Ti-dings of a gos-pel true.

poco *p cresc.*

Words reprinted by permission of Evans Brothers Ltd.

p cresc.
sempre cresc.
Swift are wing - ing An-gels sing - ing, No-wells ring - ing, Ti - dings bring-ing,
Thus re-joic - ing, Free from sor - row, Prai-ses voic - ing, Greet the mor - row,
p cresc.
sempre cresc.
Swift are wing-ing An-gels sing - ing, No-wells ring - ing, Ti - dings bring-ing,
Thus re - joic - ing, Free from sor - row, Prai-ses voic - ing, Greet the mor - row,
sempre cresc.
wing - ing An-gels sing - ing, No-wells ring - ing, Ti-dings bring-ing, Christ the
-joic - ing, Free from sor - row, Prai-ses voic - ing, Greet the mor - row, Christ the
p cresc.
sempre cresc.
Swift are wing-ing An - gels sing-ing, No - wells ring-ing, Ti - dings
Thus re- joic-ing, Free from sor-row, Prai - ses voic-ing, Greet the
sempre cresc.
mf
f
Christ the Babe is Lord of all, Christ the Babe is Lord of all.
Christ the Babe was born for you! Christ the Babe was born for you!
mf
f
Christ the Babe is Lord, Lord of all, Christ the Babe is Lord, Lord of all.
Christ the Babe was born, born for you! Christ the Babe was born, born for you!
mf
f
Babe is Lord of all, Lord of all, Christ the Babe is Lord, Lord of all.
Babe was born for you! born for you! Christ the Babe was born, born for you!
mf
f
bring-ing, Christ the Babe is Lord of all, Christ the Babe is Lord of all.
mor-row, Christ the Babe was born for you! Christ the Babe was born for you!
mf
f

17. I SAW THREE SHIPS

(First tune)

English traditional carol
arranged by DAVID WILLCOCKS

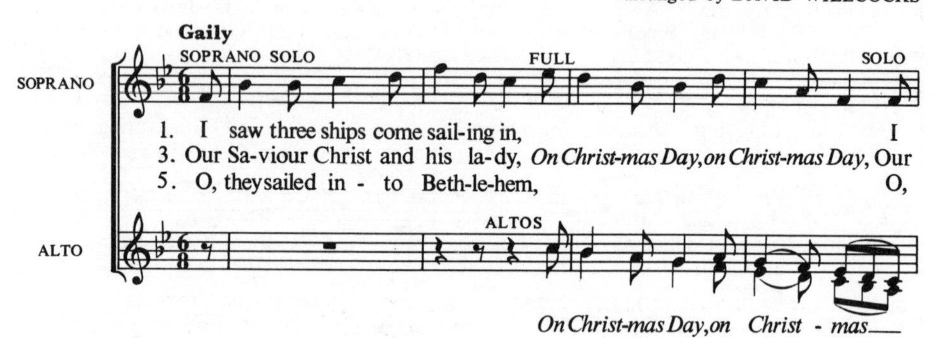

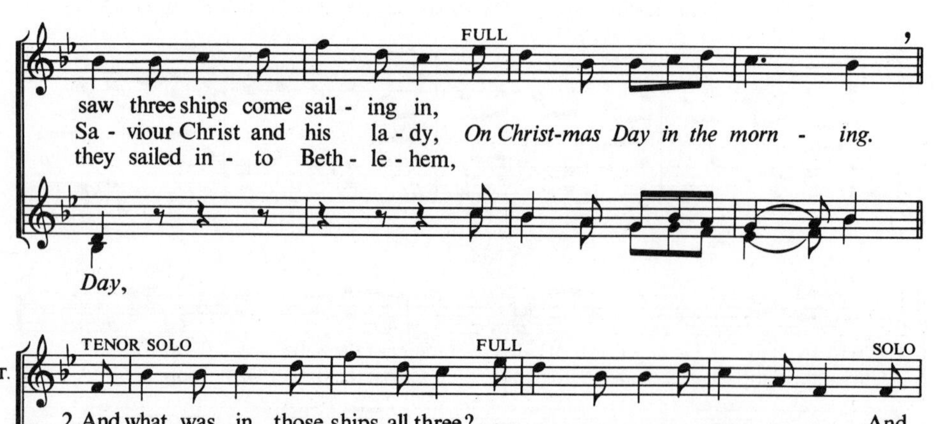

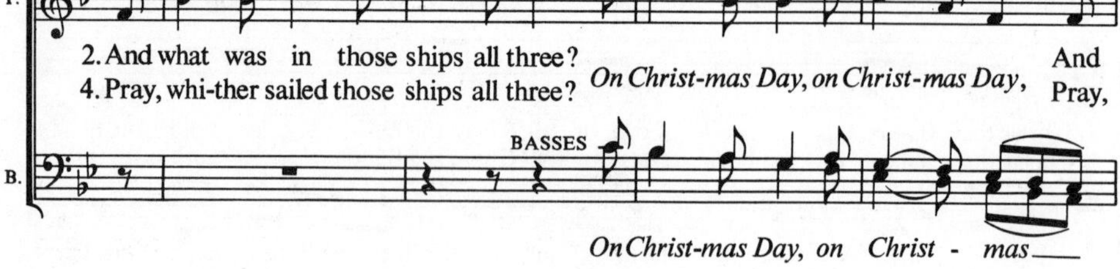

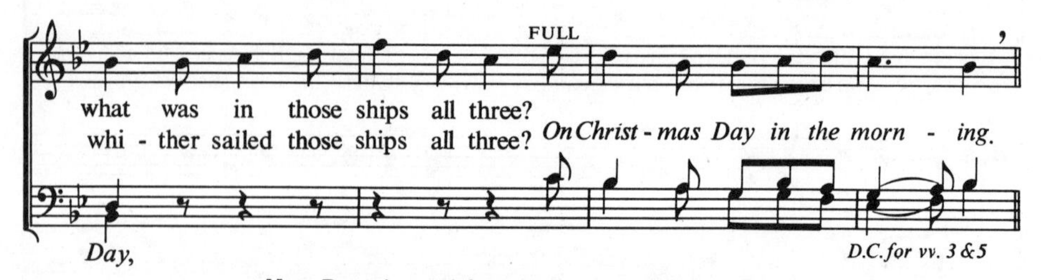

Note: Dynamics are left to the discretion of the conductor.

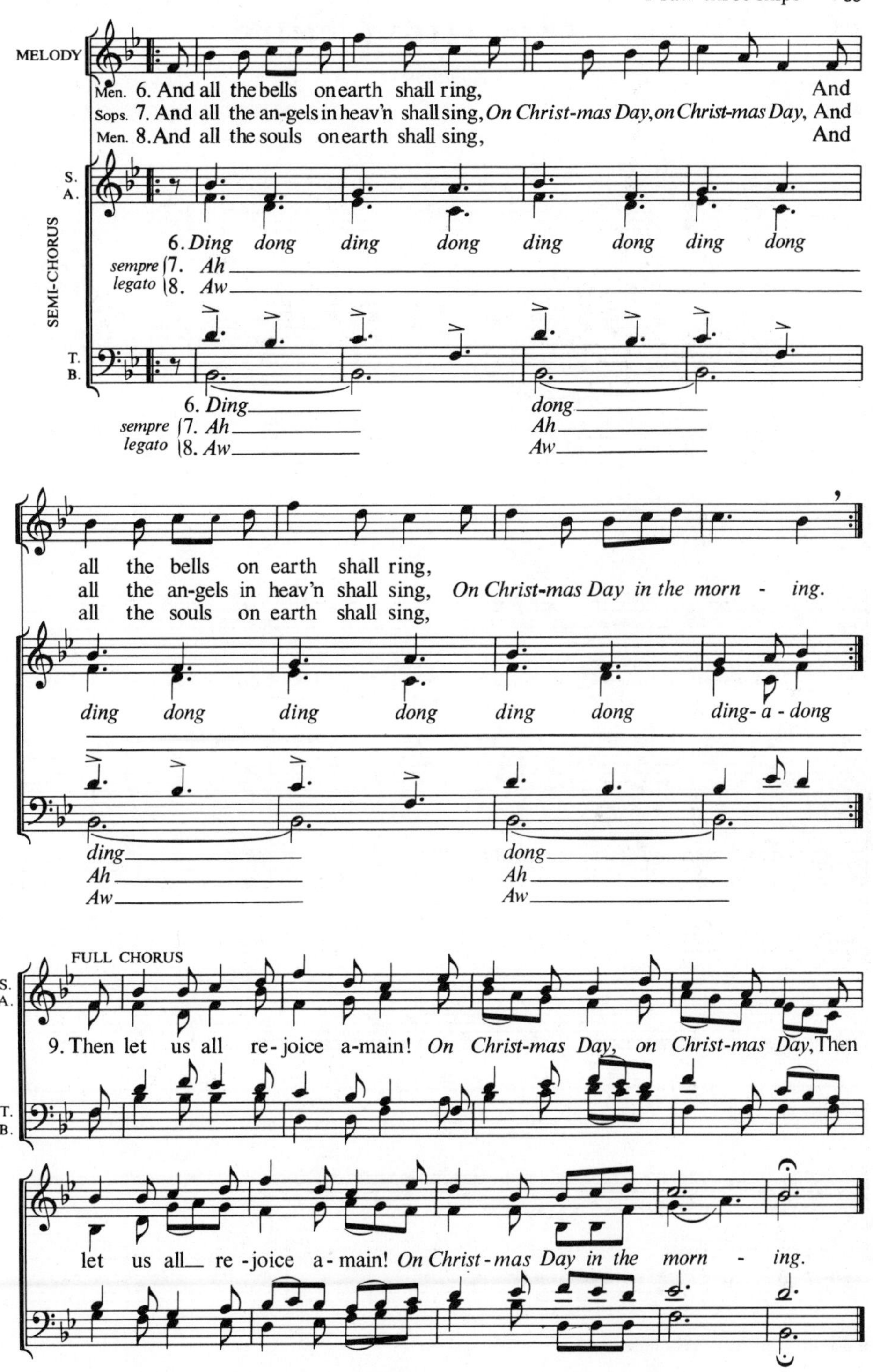
MELODY
Men. 6. And all the bells on earth shall ring, And all the bells on earth shall ring,
Sops. 7. And all the an-gels in heav'n shall sing, On Christ-mas Day, on Christ-mas Day, And all the an-gels in heav'n shall sing, On Christ-mas Day in the morn - ing.
Men. 8. And all the souls on earth shall sing, And all the souls on earth shall sing,
S. A.
SEMI-CHORUS
6. Ding dong ding dong ding dong ding dong ding dong ding dong ding dong ding-a-dong
sempre legato 7. Ah
8. Aw
T. B.
6. Ding dong ding dong
sempre legato 7. Ah Ah Ah Ah
8. Aw Aw Aw Aw
FULL CHORUS
9. Then let us all re-joice a-main! On Christ-mas Day, on Christ-mas Day, Then let us all re-joice a-main! On Christ-mas Day in the morn - ing.

17. I SAW THREE SHIPS

(Second tune)

Words traditional

REGINALD JACQUES

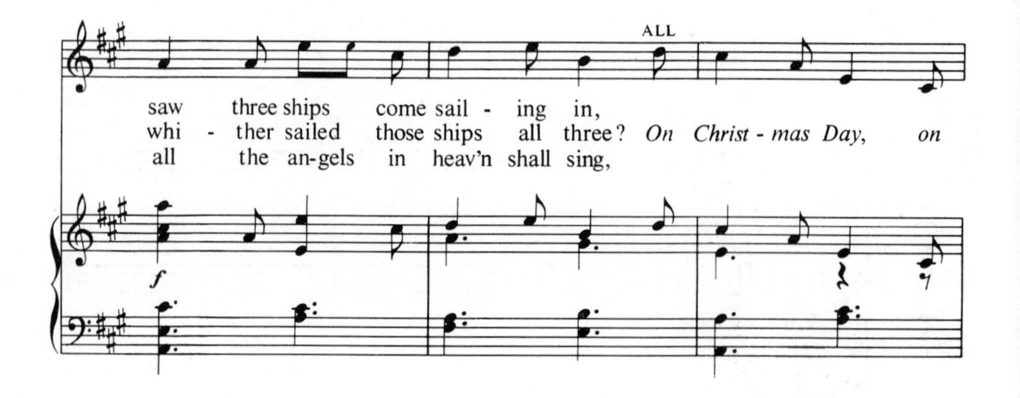

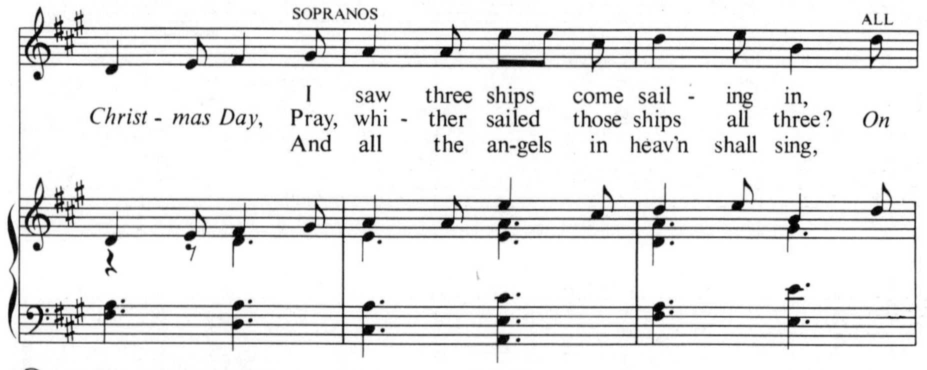

SOPRANOS
mf
2. And what was in those
Christ - mas Day in the morn - ing. 5. O, they sailed in - to
8. And all the souls on
mf
ALL
SOPRANOS
ships all three? And
Beth - le - hem, On Christ - mas Day, on Christ - mas Day, O,
earth shall sing, And
ALL
what was in those ships all three?
they sailed in - to Beth - le - hem, On Christ - mas Day in the
all the souls on earth shall sing,

SOPRANOS
f
3. Our Sa - viour Christ and his la - dy,
morn - ing. 6. And all the bells on earth shall ring, On
9. Then let us all re - joice a - main!
f

SOPRANOS
Our Sa - viour Christ and
Christ - mas Day, on Christ - mas Day, And all the bells on
Then let us all re -

ALL
D.C.
his la - dy,
earth shall ring, On Christ - mas Day in the morn - ing.
- joice a - main!
(Last time only)
(Last time only)

18. IT CAME UPON THE MIDNIGHT CLEAR

Words by
E.H. SEARS

Traditional English tune
adapted by ARTHUR SULLIVAN

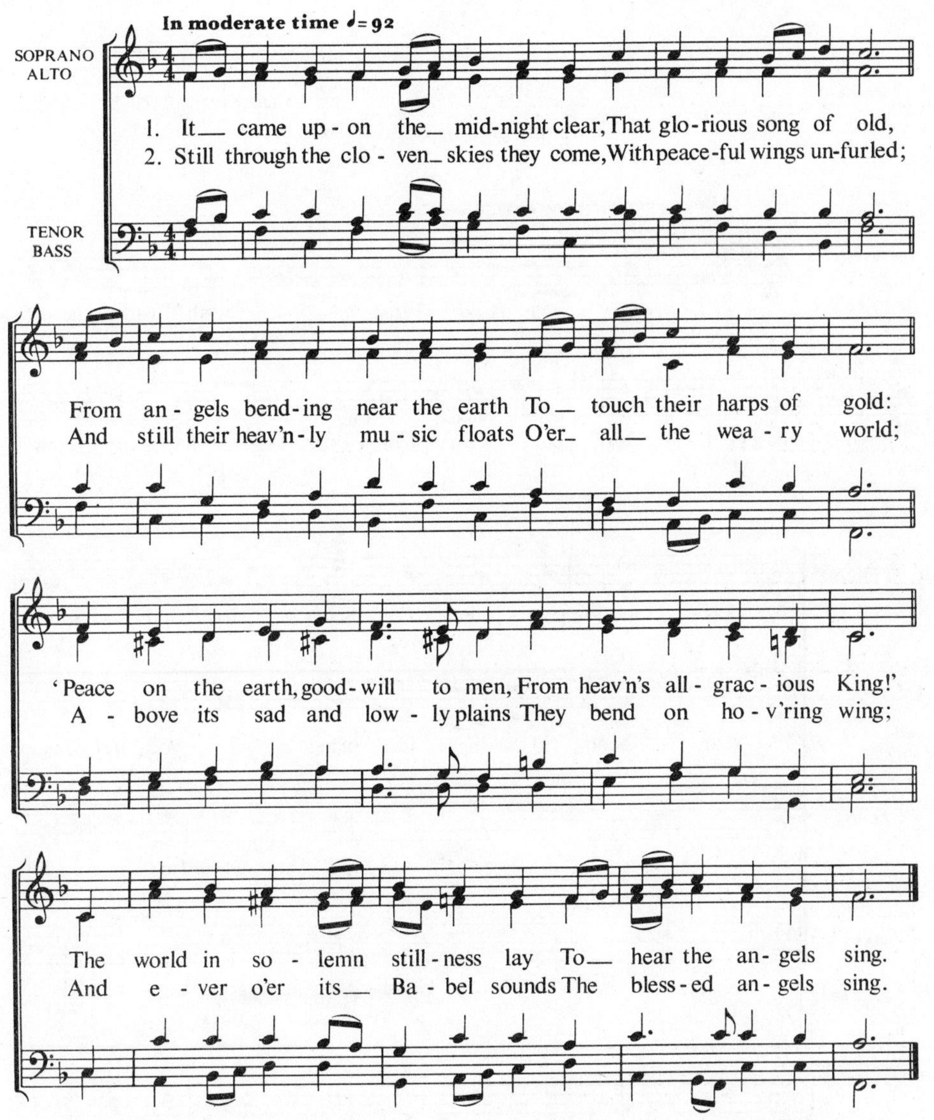
In moderate time ♩= 92
SOPRANO
ALTO
TENOR
BASS
1. It_ came up-on the_ mid-night clear, That glo-rious song of old,
2. Still through the clo - ven_ skies they come, With peace-ful wings un-furled;
From an-gels bend-ing near the earth To_ touch their harps of gold:
And still their heav'n-ly mu-sic floats O'er_ all_ the wea-ry world;
'Peace on the earth, good-will to men, From heav'n's all-grac-ious King!'
A-bove its sad and low-ly plains They bend on ho-v'ring wing;
The world in so-lemn still-ness lay To_ hear the an-gels sing.
And e-ver o'er its_ Ba-bel sounds The bless-ed an-gels sing.

3. Yet with the woes of sin and strife
   The world has suffered long;
Beneath the angel-strain have rolled
   Two thousand years of wrong;
And man, at war with man, hears not
   The love-song which they bring:
O hush the noise, ye men of strife,
   And hear the angels sing!

4. For lo! the days are hastening on,
   By prophet-bards foretold,
When, with the ever-circling years,
   Comes round the age of gold;
When peace shall over all the earth
   Its ancient splendours fling,
And the whole world send back the song
   Which now the angels sing.

To Geoffrey Shaw

19. A MERRY CHRISTMAS

Traditional (West country) carol
arranged by ARTHUR WARRELL

kin; I (We) wish you a mer-ry Christ-mas And a hap - py New
kin; I (We) wish you a mer-ry Christ-mas And a hap - py New
bring; I (We) wish you a mer-ry Christ-mas And a hap - py New
bring; I (We) wish you a mer-ry Christ - mas And a hap - py New
Year.
Year.
Year. Now bring us some fig-gy pud - ding, Now bring us some fig-gy
Year. Now bring us some fig-gy pud - ding, Now

pud - ding, Now bring us some fig-gy pud - ding, And bring some out
bring us some fig-gy pud - ding, Now bring us fig-gy pud - ding out
Good tid - ings I bring To you and your
(We)
Good tid - ings I bring To you and your kin; I
(We) (We)
here. Good tid - ings I bring To you and your kin; I
(We) (We)
here. Good tid - ings I bring To you and your kin; I
(We) (We)

mf
f
kin; A hap - - - - - - - py New Year. For we
wish you a mer-ry Christ-mas And a hap - py New Year. For we
wish you a hap - py New Year. For we
wish you a mer-ry Christ-mas And a hap - py New Year. For we
all like fig-gy pud - ding, We all like fig-gy pud - ding, For we
all like fig-gy pud - ding, We all like fig-gy pud - ding, For we
all like fig-gy pud - ding, For we all like fig- gy pud-ding, For we
all like fig - - - gy pud - ding, For we

all like– fig-gy pud - ding, So bring some out here. Good tid - ings I
(We)
all like– fig-gy pud-ding, So bring some, so bring some out here. Good
all– like– fig-gy pud - ding, So bring some out here.
all like fig-gy pud - ding, So bring some, bring some out here. Good–
bring To you and your kin; I wish you a mer-ry
(We)
tid - ings I– bring to– your kin; I wish you a mer-ry
(We) (We)
Good– tid - ings I– bring to your kin; I
(We) (We)
tid - ings I bring to your kin;– I wish you a mer-ry
(We) (We)

Christ- mas And a hap - py New Year. And we won't go,
Christ-mas And a hap - py— New Year. And we won't go— till we've
wish you a hap- py New Year.— And we won't go,
Christ - mas And a hap- py— New Year. —— And we won't go,
won't go, won't go, won't go, And we won't go till we've
got some, We won't go,— till we've got some, And we won't go— till we've
won't go, won't go, won't go, And we won't go till we've
won't go, won't go, won't go, And we won't go till we've

got_some, So bring some out here. Good tid - ings I bring To
(We)
got some, So bring some out here. Good tid - ings_ I__ bring To
(We)
got some, So bring some out here. Good tid - ings_ I__ bring To
(We)
got some, So bring some out here. Good_ tid - ings I bring__ To_
(We)
you and your kin; I wish you a mer-ry Christ - mas And a
(We)
you and_your kin; I wish you a mer- ry Christ-mas And a
(We)
you and your kin;__ I wish you a mer- ry Christ - mas And a
(We)
you and your_ kin;__ I wish you a mer-ry Christ - mas_ And a
(We)

accel.
molto rall.
hap - py New Year, A hap - py New Year, I (We)
hap - py New Year, A hap - py New Year, I (We)
hap - py New Year, A hap - py New Year, I (We)
hap - py New Year, A hap - py New Year, I (We)
wish you a mer-ry Christ - mas And a hap - py New Year.
wish you a mer-ry Christ - mas And a hap - py New Year.
wish you a mer-ry Christ - mas And a hap - py New Year.
wish you a mer-ry Christ - mas And a hap - py New Year.

20. KING JESUS HATH A GARDEN

Tr. G.R. WOODWARD

Dutch tune
harmonized by CHARLES WOOD

SOPRANO
ALTO
TENOR
BASS
1. King Je - sus hath a gar-den, full of di - vers flow'rs, Where
2. The Li - ly, white in blos-som there, is Chas - ti - ty: The
I go cull - ing po - sies gay, all times__ and__ hours.
Vi - o - let, with sweet per - fume, Hu - mi - li - ty.
There
naught is heard but Pa - ra - dise bird, Harp, dul - ci - mer, lute, With
cym - bal,__ trump and tym - bal, And the ten - der,_ sooth - ing flute; With

Reprinted from *The Cowley Carol Book* by permission

cym - bal, — trump and tym-bal, And the ten - der, — sooth-ing flute. —

3. The bonny Damask-rose is known as Patïence:
   The blithe and thrifty Marygold, Obedïence.

   There naught is heard, etc.

4. The Crown Imperial bloometh too in yonder place,
   'Tis Charity, of stock divine, the flower of grace.

   There naught is heard, etc.

5. Yet, 'mid the brave, the bravest prize of all may claim‿
   The Star of Bethlem – Jesus – blessèd be his Name!

   There naught is heard, etc.

6. Ah! Jesu Lord, my heal and weal, my bliss complete,
   Make thou my heart thy garden-plot, fair, trim and neat.
   That I may hear this musick clear:
   Harp, dulcimer, lute,
   With cymbal, trump and tymbal,
   And the tender, soothing flute.

21. ROCKING

Tr. PERCY DEARMER

Czech carol
arranged by DAVID WILLCOCKS

Words and melody from *The Oxford Book of Carols*, by permission

rock you, rock you, We will rock you, rock you, rock you: See the fur to
We will serve you
lul - la - by, lul - la, lul - la - by,
lul - la - by, lul - la, lul - la, lul - la - by, lul - la -
lul - la - by, lul - la, lul - la - by, lul - la - by,
lul - la - by, lul - la, lul - la - by, lul - la -
keep you warm, Snug - ly round your ti - ny form.
all we can, Dar - ling, dar - ling lit - tle man.
lul - la - by, lul - la, lul - la, lul - la - by.
- by, lul - la, lul - la, lul - la, lul - la - by.
lul - la - by, lul - la, lul - la, lul - la - by.
- by, lul - la, lul - la, lul - la, lul - la - by.

22. CAROL, WITH LULLABY

Words anon.
(adapted by PHYLLIS TATE)

PHYLLIS TATE

pp
cresc.
lul - la, lul - la - by. My sweet lit - tle ba - - by, what
pp
cresc.
lul - - lul - la - by. My sweet lit - tle ba - - by, what
pp
cresc.
mf
mean - est thou to cry? A King is born, they say, which
mf
mean - est thou to cry? A King is born, they say, which
mp
mf
What mean - est thou to cry,
mf

mp
King a king would kill; Oh wo, oh wo, oh
King a king would kill; Oh wo, oh wo, oh
cry? Oh wo, oh wo, oh
mf
A king would kill; Oh wo, oh wo, oh
cresc.
wo - ful, hea - vy day, oh hea - - vy day when
wo - ful, hea - vy day, oh hea - - vy day when
wo - ful, hea - vy day, oh hea - - vy day when
wo - ful, hea - vy day, oh hea - - vy day when

dim. molto
mp e poco rall.
pp a tempo
wretch-es have their will, when wretch-es have their will.
wretch-es have their will, their will.
wretch-es have their will, have their will.
wretch-es have their will, their will.
mp poco rall
pp a tempo
mp
And
And
And
pp
Lul - la, lul - la,
p

p
shep-herds heard the song which an - gels bright did sing, All
shep-herds heard the song which an - gels bright did sing, All
shep-herds heard the song which an - gels bright did sing, All
(pp)
lul - la, lul - la, lul - la, lul - la, lul - la, lul - la, lul - la, lul - la,
8
cresc.
giv - ing glo - ry un - to God, for com - ing of this King, this
mf
giv - ing glo - ry un - to God, for com - ing of this King; Which
f
giv - ing glo - ry un - to God, for com - ing of this King; Which
mp
lul - la, lul - la, lul - la, lul - la, lul - la, lul - la, lul - la - by, this

King, this King;
must be made a - way, King Her - od would him kill.
must be made a - way, King Her - od would him kill.
mf
King, this King; Oh
8
mf
mp
Wo, wo, wo - ful, hea - vy day, oh
(mp)
Wo, wo, wo - ful, hea - vy day, oh
Wo, wo, wo - ful, hea - vy day, oh
mf
Wo, oh wo, oh wo - ful, hea - vy day, oh
mp

cresc.
f
molto dim. e
hea - - vy day when wretch-es have their will, when wretch-es
cresc.
f
molto dim. e
hea - - vy day when wretch-es have their will, their
cresc.
f
molto dim. e
hea - - vy day when wretch-es have their will,
cresc.
f
molto dim. e
hea - - vy day when wretch-es have their will,
cresc.
f

a tempo ma piu marcato
poco rall.
pp
mf
have their will. And thou shalt live and
poco rall.
pp
mf
will. And thou shalt live and
poco rall.
pp
mf
have their will. And thou shalt
poco rall.
pp
mf
their will. And thou shalt
a tempo ma piu marcato
poco rall.
mp
pp
f

reign, shalt live and reign, As all the pro-phets
reign who was in a man-ger laid, As all the pro-phets
reign who was in a man-ger laid, As all the pro-phets
reign, shalt live and reign, As all the pro-phets
8
f
pro-phe-sy, as sy-bils have fore-said; Whom cai-tiffs ne'er be-
f
pro-phe-sy, as sy-bils have fore-said; Whom cai-tiffs ne'er be-
f
pro-phe-sy, as sy-bils have fore-said; Whom cai-tiffs ne'er be-
f
pro-phe-sy, as sy-bils have fore-said; Whom cai-tiffs ne'er be-

mf
mf
-tray, whom ty - rants none can kill; Oh joy, oh
f
f
-tray, whom ty - rants none can kill; Oh joy, oh
mf
mf
-tray, whom ty - rants none can kill; Oh joy, oh
mf
mf
-tray, whom ty - rants none can kill; Oh joy, oh
mf
mf
cresc.
joy, oh joy - ful, hap - py day, oh hap - - py
f
mf
cresc.
joy, oh joy - ful, hap - py day, oh hap - - py
mf
cresc.
joy, oh joy - ful, hap - py day, oh hap - - py
mf
cresc.
joy, oh joy - ful, hap - py day, oh hap - - py
mf
mf
mf
cresc.

poco allargando
a tempo
f
day when wretch - es want their will, when
day when wretch - es want their will, when wretch - es
day when wretch - es want their will, when wretch - es
day when wretch - es want their will,
f a tempo
mf
ff
wretch - es want their will.
want their will.
want their will.
want their will.
8

23. COVENTRY CAROL

(First version)

Pageant of the Shearmen and Tailors, 15th century

Original tune of 1591

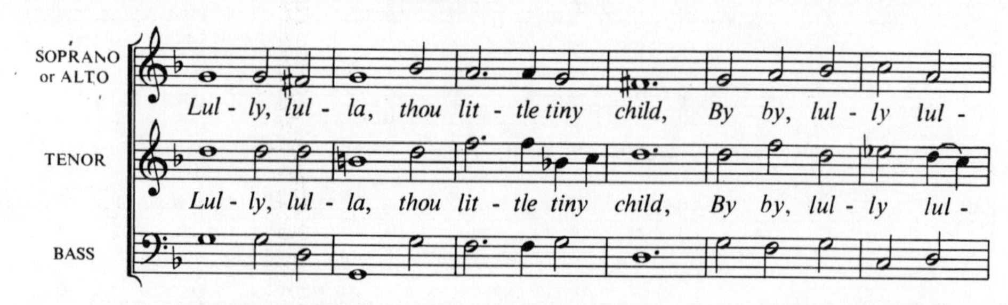

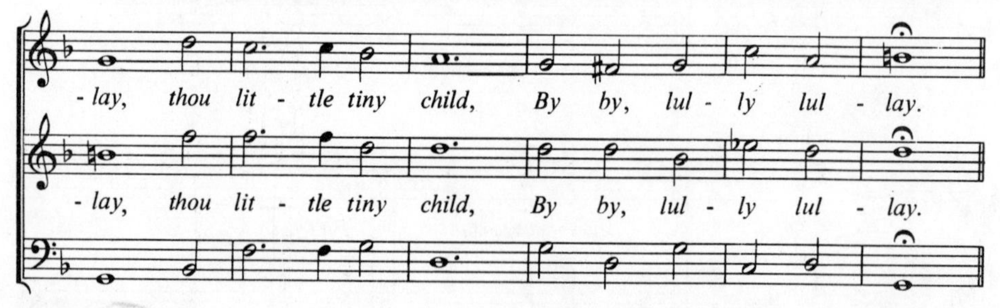

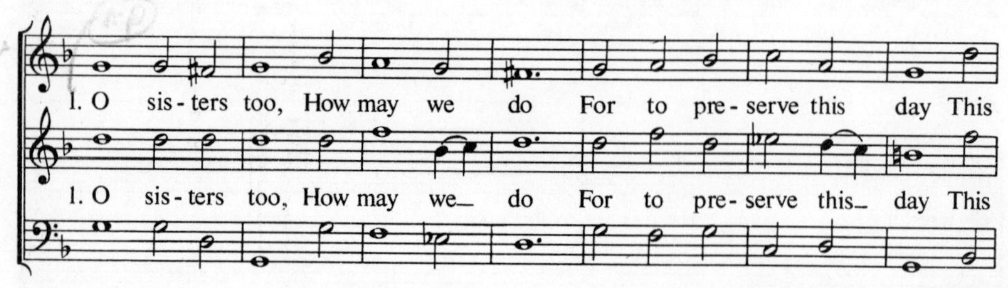

The above Refrain and First Verse is scored from the original.

2. Herod, the king,
In his raging,
Chargèd he hath this day
His men of might,
In his own sight,
All young childrén to slay.

3. That woe is me,
Poor child for thee!
And ever morn and day,
For thy parting
Neither say nor sing
By by, lully lullay!

This song is sung by the women of Bethlehem in the play, just before Herod's soldiers come in to slaughter their children.

* The original manuscript has F and D in tenor part here.

23. COVENTRY CAROL

(Second version)

Modern version of tune
arranged by MARTIN SHAW

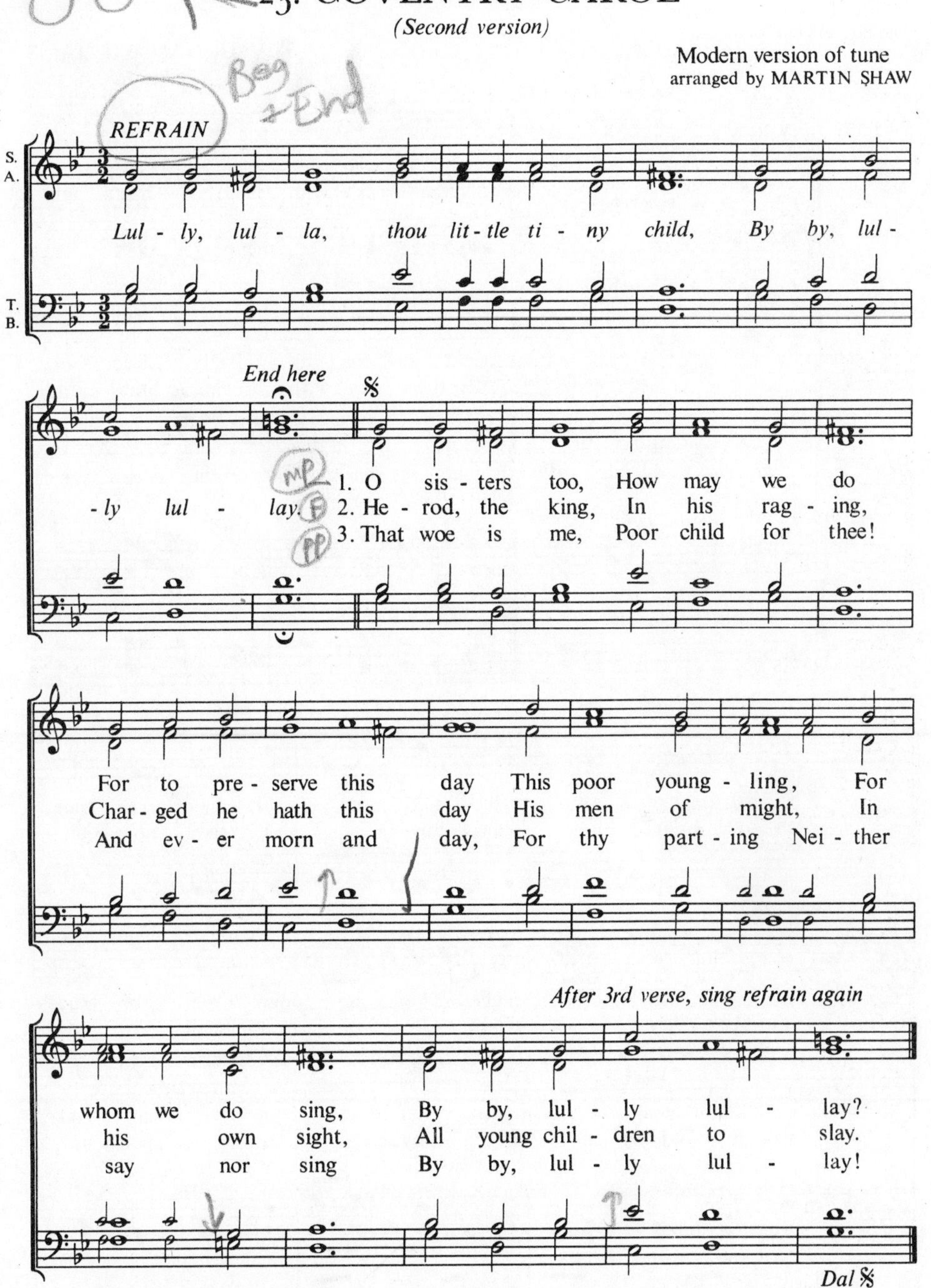

This song is sung by the women of Bethlehem in the play, just before Herod's soldiers come in to slaughter their children.

24. NO SAD THOUGHT HIS SOUL AFFRIGHT

Words:
Verse 1. Anon.
Verse 2. URSULA VAUGHAN WILLIAMS*

R. VAUGHAN WILLIAMS

Lento (𝅗𝅥 = 66)

sempre **pp**

SOPRANO
1. No sad thought his soul af - fright, Sleep it
2. fills the sky with light, Stars and

ALTO

TENOR
1. No sad thought his soul af - fright,_ Sleep it
2. fills the sky with light,_ Stars and

BASS
1. No sad thought his soul af - fright,_ Sleep it
2. fills the sky with light,_ Stars and

Lento (𝅗𝅥 = 66)

(for practice only)

pp

is that mak - eth night; Let no_ mur - mur nor rude
an - gels dance in flight; Joy of_ heav'n shall now un -

is that_ mak - eth_ night;_ Let_ no_ mur - mur nor rude_
an - gels_ dance in_ flight;_ Joy_ of_ heav'n shall now un -

is that mak - eth_ night; Let_ no rude_
an - gels dance in_ flight; Joy_ shall un -

*By permission

Reprinted from the cantata *Hodie* (O.U.P.)

†pronounce 'wind' to rhyme with 'kind'

wake To as ma - ny joys as can In this
sake; Nev - er since the world be - gan Such a
wake To as ma - ny joys as can In this
sake; Nev - er since the world be - gan Such a
wake To as ma - ny joys as can In this
sake; Nev - er since the world be - gan Such a
(♩=♩)
ppp pp ppp
world be - fall a man. 2. Pro - mise span.
light such dark did
world be - fall a man. 2. Pro - mise span.
light such dark did
world be - fall a man. 2. Pro - mise span.
light such dark did

25. O LITTLE ONE SWEET

Tr. PERCY DEARMER

Old German tune
harmonized by J. S. BACH

Rather slowly
SOPRANO
ALTO
TENOR
BASS
1. O lit - tle one sweet, O lit - tle one mild, Thy Fa - ther's pur - pose thou hast ful - filled; Thou cam'st from heav'n to mor - tal ken, E - qual to be with us poor men, O lit - tle one sweet, O lit - tle one mild.
2. O lit - tle one sweet, O lit - tle one mild, With joy thou hast the whole world filled; Thou cam - est here from heav'n's do - main, To bring men com - fort in their pain, O lit - tle one sweet, O lit - tle one mild.

3. O little one sweet, O little one mild,
In thee Love's beauties are all distilled;
Then light in us thy love's bright flame,
That we may give thee back the same,
O little one sweet, O little one mild.

4. O little one sweet, O little one mild,
Help us to do as thou hast willed.
Lo, all we have belongs to thee!
Ah, keep us in our fealty!
O little one sweet, O little one mild.

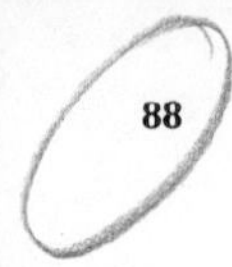

26. O COME, ALL YE FAITHFUL

(ADESTE FIDELES)

Tr. F. OAKELEY, W. T. BROOKE and others

Composer unknown (probably 18th c.)
arranged by DAVID WILLCOCKS

SOPRANO
ALTO
(ORGAN)
TENOR
BASS
1. O come, all ye faith - ful, Joy - ful and tri - um - phant, O come ye, O come ye to Beth - le - hem;
2. God of God, Light of Light, Lo! he ab - hors not the Vir - gin's womb;
Come and be - hold him Born the King of An - gels:
Ve - ry God, Be - got - ten, not cre - a - ted:
Man.
O come, let us a - dore him, O come, let us a - dore him, O
Ped.
come, let us a - dore him, Christ the Lord!

Note: Verses 1-5 may be sung by unison voices and organ, S.A.T.B. voices and organ, or voices unaccompanied as desired. Verses 3-5 may be omitted. The harmonies used for vv. 1-5 are from *The English Hymnal*.

3. See how the shepherds,
Summoned to his cradle,
Leaving their flocks, draw nigh with lowly fear;
We too will thither
Bend our joyful footsteps:
O come, etc.

4. Lo! star-led chieftains,
Magi, Christ adoring,
Offer him incense, gold and myrrh;
We to the Christ Child
Bring our hearts' oblations:
O come, etc.

5. Child, for us sinners
Poor and in the manger,
Fain we embrace thee, with awe and love;
Who would not love thee,
Loving us so dearly?
O come, etc.

ff
Glo - - - - - - - - - - - - ry in the high - est:
ff
Glo - ry to God In the high - est: O
mf
ff
mf
mf
O come,
come, let us a - dore him, O come, let us a - dore him, O
cresc.
f
O come,
f
cresc.
f
cresc.
let us a - dore him, Christ the Lord.
cresc.
come, let us a - dore him, Christ the Lord.
ff
cresc.
ff
ff

All voices
f
7. Yea, Lord, we greet thee, Born this hap-py morn - ing, Je - su, to
f Gt. + Full Sw.
thee be glo - ry giv'n; Word of the Fa - ther,
ff
ff
Now in flesh ap-pear - ing: O come, let us a - dore him, O come, let us a-
p
mf
p
mf
Man.
-dore him, O come, let us a - dore him, Christ the Lord!
ff
ff
Ped.

27. O LITTLE TOWN OF BETHLEHEM

Words by BISHOP PHILLIPS BROOKS

English traditional tune
arranged by R. VAUGHAN WILLIAMS.
Descant by THOMAS ARMSTRONG

SOPRANO
ALTO

(ORGAN
or
PIANO)

TENOR
BASS

1. O lit - tle town of Beth- le - hem, How still we see thee lie!
2. O morn-ing stars, to - geth - er Pro- claim the ho - ly birth,
3. How si - lent - ly, how si - lent - ly, The won-drous gift is giv'n!

A - bove thy deep and dream-less sleep The si - lent stars go by.
And prais - es sing to God the King, And peace to men on earth;
So God im-parts to hu - man hearts The bless - ings of his heav'n.

Yet in thy dark streets shin - eth The ev - er - last - ing light;
For Christ is born of Ma - - ry; And, gath-ered all a - bove,
No ear may hear his com - - ing; But in this world of sin,

The hopes and fears of all the years Are met in thee to - night.
While mor-tals sleep, the an - gels keep Their watch of wond-'ring love.
Where meek souls will re - ceive him, still The dear Christ en - ters in.

Descant reprinted by permission of The Royal School of Church Music

DESCANT
Sop
4. O ho-ly_Child of Beth-le-hem, Des-cend to us, we pray!
UNISON VOICES
ORGAN or PIANO
Cast out our_ sin, and en-ter in, Be born in us to-day.
We_ hear the Christ-mas an - gels The great glad ti - dings tell:
O come to_ us, a - bide with us, Our Lord Em-man-u - el.

28. O MEN FROM THE FIELDS

A CRADLE SONG

(Solo or unison voices)

Words by
PADRAIC COLUM

ARNOLD COOKE

Allegretto
(Voices in unison)
VOICE(S)
PIANO
or
ORGAN
O men from the fields! Come gen-tly with-in. Tread soft - ly, soft-ly, O men com-ing in!
Ma-vour-neen is go-ing From me and from you, Where Ma-ry will fold him With man-tle of blue!

Words reprinted by permission

(Solo)
mf
From reek of the smoke, And cold of the
mf
(Unison)
p
floor, And the peer-ing of things A-cross the half-door. O
men from the fields! Soft, soft-ly come through— Ma-ry puts
round him Her man-tle of blue.
dim.
pp

Homage to R.V.W.

29. SUSSEX CAROL

English traditional carol
arranged by DAVID WILLCOCKS

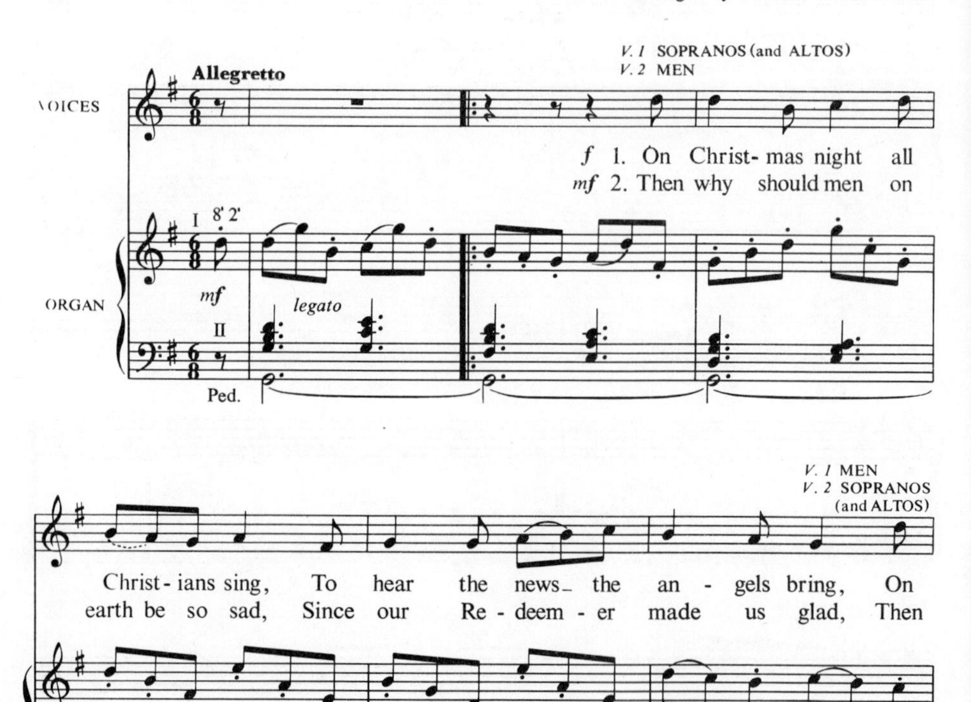

Christ - mas night all Christ-ians sing, To hear the news the an-gels bring–
why should men on earth be so sad, Since our Re-deem-er made us glad,

Melody and words reprinted by permission of Ursula Vaughan Williams

1st time (v.1)
SOPRANOS (and ALTOS)
News of great joy, news of great mirth,
FULL
News of our mer - ci - ful King's birth.
2nd time (v.2)
S.
A.
p (Voices unaccompanied)
When from our sin he set us free,
T.
B.
p
(Organ tacet)
All for to gain our lib - er - ty?
2
ORGAN

CHOIR I
(melody)
mf
3. When sin de-parts be-fore his grace, Then life and health come
CHOIR II
1st time mf Ah
2nd time p
(Voices unaccompanied)
1st time
2nd time
p
cresc.
in its place; When in its place; An-gels and men with joy may
cresc.
An-gels and men with
cresc.
f
sing, All for to see the new-born King.
joy may sing, All for to see the new-born King.
Gt.
Full. Sw.
ORGAN

CHOIRS I & II
S.
A.
T. & B. (melody)
f
ff
Ah
4. All out of dark - ness we have light, Which made the an - gels
stacc.
2nd time cresc.
1st time
2nd time
'Glo - ry to God and
sing this night: All sing this night: 'Glo - ry to God and peace to
peace to men, Now and for ev - er - more. A - men'.
men, Now and for ev - er - more. A - men'.
poco rall.

30. ONCE IN ROYAL DAVID'S CITY

Words by C.F. ALEXANDER

H.J. GAUNTLETT
harmonized by A.H. MANN

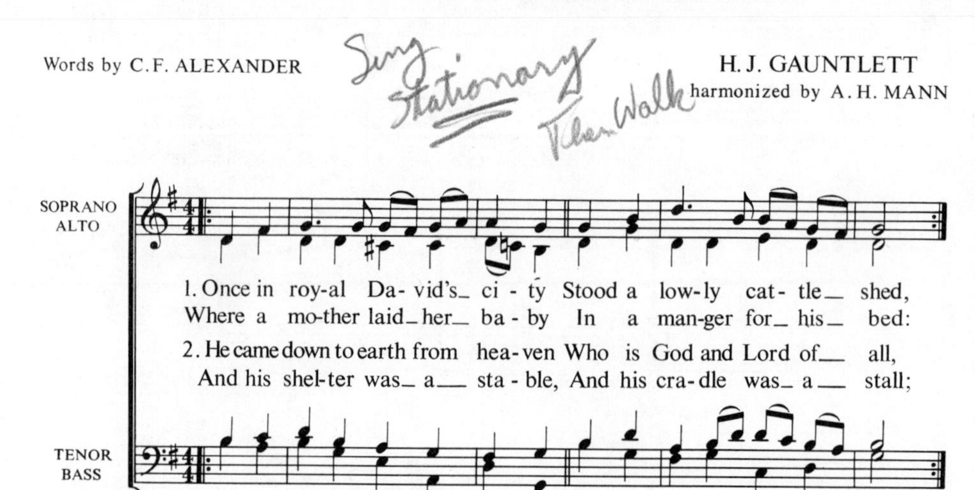
SOPRANO
ALTO
TENOR
BASS
1. Once in roy-al Da- vid's_ ci - ty Stood a low-ly cat- tle_ shed,
Where a mo-ther laid_her_ ba - by In a man-ger for_ his_ bed:
2. He came down to earth from hea-ven Who is God and Lord of_ all,
And his shel-ter was_ a_ sta - ble, And his cra- dle was_ a_ stall;

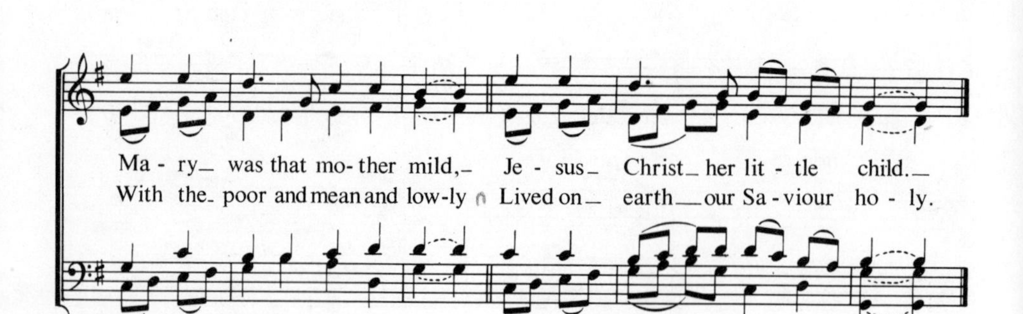
Ma - ry_ was that mo- ther mild,_ Je - sus_ Christ_ her lit - tle child._
With the_ poor and mean and low-ly Lived on_ earth_our Sa - viour ho - ly.

3. And through all his wondrous childhood
He would honour and obey,
Love and watch the lowly maiden,
In whose gentle arms he lay:
Christian children all must be
Mild, obedient, good as he.

4. For he is our childhood's pattern,
Day by day like us he grew,
He was little, weak, and helpless,
Tears and smiles like us he knew:
And he feeleth for our sadness,
And he shareth in our gladness.

5. And our eyes at last shall see him,
Through his own redeeming love,
For that child so dear and gentle
Is our Lord in heaven above;
And he leads his children on
To the place where he is gone.

6. Not in that poor lowly stable,
With the oxen standing by,
We shall see him; but in heaven,
Set at God's right hand on high;
Where like stars his children crowned
All in white shall wait around.

31. PAST THREE A CLOCK

Words by
G. R. WOODWARD

Traditional carol
harmonized by CHARLES WOOD

SOPRANO
ALTO
TENOR
BASS
Past three a clock, And a cold fro-sty morn - ing: Past three a clock; Good
mor-row, mas-ters all!
Fine
1. Born is a ba - by, Gen-tle as may be,
2. Se - raph quire sing - eth, An-gel bell ring - eth:
Son — of — th' e - ter - nal Fa - ther su - per - nal.
Hark — how — they rime — it, Time it, and chime it.
Past three a clock,

3. Mid earth rejoices
Hearing such voices
Ne'ertofore so well
Carolling *Nowell.*
Past three a clock, etc.

4. Hinds o'er the pearly
Dewy lawn early
Seek the high stranger
Laid in the manger.
Past three a clock, etc.

5. Cheese from the dairy
Bring they for Mary,
And, not for money,
Butter and honey.
Past three a clock, etc.

6. Light out of star-land
Leadeth from far land
Princes, to meet him,
Worship and greet him.
Past three a clock, etc.

7. Myrrh from full coffer,
Incense they offer:
Nor is the golden
Nugget withholden.
Past three a clock, etc.

8. Thus they: I pray you,
Up, sirs, nor stay you
Till ye confess him
Likewise, and bless him.
Past three a clock, etc.

The refrain *Past three a clock* is old, but the other words are by G. R. W. The tune is *London Waits*, from W. Chappell's *Popular Music of the Olden Time.*

32. REJOICE AND BE MERRY

(A GALLERY CAROL)

English traditional carol
arranged by REGINALD JACQUES

SOPRANO
ALTO
TENOR
BASS
1. Re - joice and be mer - ry in songs and in mirth! O praise our Re-deem-er, all mor-tals on earth! For this is the birth-day of Je - sus our King, Who brought us sal - va - tion–his prai-ses we'll sing!
2. A hea - ven - ly vi - sion ap - peared in the sky; Vast num - bers of an - gels the shep-herds did spy, Pro - claim-ing the birth-day of Je - sus our King, Who brought us sal - va - tion–his prai-ses we'll sing!

3. Likewise a bright star in the sky did appear,
Which led the wise men from the east to draw near;
They found the Messiah, sweet Jesus our King,
Who brought us salvation—his praises we'll sing!

4. And when they were come, they their treasures unfold,
And unto him offered myrrh, incense, and gold.
So blessèd for ever be Jesus our King,
Who brought us salvation—his praises we'll sing!

The words and tune, from an old church-gallery book discovered in Dorset, reprinted from *The Oxford Book of Carols* by permission

33. SEE AMID THE WINTER'S SNOW

Words by E. CASWALL

JOHN GOSS
arranged by DAVID WILLCOCKS

SOLO or FULL SOPRANOS
ORGAN
p
p dolce
Man.
Ped.
1. See a-mid the win-ter's snow, Born for us on earth be-low; See the ten-der Lamb ap-pears, Pro-mis'd from e - ter - nal years:
CHORUS
f
S.
A.
CHORUS and ORGAN
Hail, thou e - ver - bless-ed morn; Hail, re-demp-tion's hap-py dawn;
T.
B.
Sing through all Je - ru - sa - lem, Christ is born in Beth - le - hem.

The harmonizations used for the refrain in verses 1, 3, and 4 are Goss's own.

CHOIR I
(or audience)
CHOIR II
(or S.A.T.B. Choir)
with
ORGAN
ad lib.
mp 2. Lo, with-in a man-ger lies He who built the star-ry skies;
pp 5. Sa - cred in-fant, all di-vine, What a ten-der love was thine,
mp 2. Lo, with-in a man-ger lies He who built the star-ry skies;
pp 5. Sa-cred in-fant, all di - vine, What a ten - der love was thine,
He who, throned in height sub-lime, Sits a-mid the che - ru-bim:
Thus to come from high - est bliss Down to such a world as this:
He who, throned in height sub - lime, Sits a - mid the che - ru - bim:
Thus to come from high - est bliss Down to such a world as this:
mf cresc.
f cresc.
Hail, thou e - ver - bless-ed morn; Hail, re-demp-tion's hap-py dawn;
Hail, thou e - ver - bless-ed morn; Hail, re-demp-tion's hap-py dawn;
Sing
ff
C2

after verse 5 to page 106 for last verse
Sing through all Je - ru - sa-lem, Christ is born in Beth - le - hem.
Sing through all Je - ru - sa - lem, Christ is born in Beth-le - hem.
Je - ru - sa- lem, Christ
SOPRANOS
3. Say, ye ho - ly shep - herds, say What your joy - ful news to-day;
ALTOS I & II (or S. II & A.)
3. Say, ye ho- ly shep-herds, say What your joy - ful news to - day;
Where- fore have ye left your sheep On the lone - ly moun - tain steep?
Where - fore have ye left your sheep On the lone - - ly moun-tain steep?
CHORUS
S. A.
Hail, thou e - ver - bless- ed morn; Hail, re - demp-tion's hap - py dawn;
T. B.
f (organ ad lib.)
Sing through all Je - ru - sa - lem, Christ is born in Beth - le - hem.

4. 'As we watch'd at dead of night, Lo, we saw a won-drous light;
TENORS I & II
pp
cresc.
4. 'As we watch'd at dead of night, Lo, we saw a won-drous
p
cresc.
f
BASSES
4. 'As we watch'd at dead of night, Lo, we saw a wondrous light; An-gels sing-ing
mf An - gels sing-ing, Told us of the Sa-viour's birth:'
cresc.
CHORUS
S. f
mf cresc.
A.
light: An - gels sing-ing of the Sa-viour's birth:'
Hail, thou e - ver - bless-ed morn;
T.
"Peace on earth" Told us of the Sa-viour's birth:'
B. f (organ ad lib.)
to 𝄋 (p. 104)
for verse 5
Hail, re-demp-tion's hap-py dawn; Sing through all Je - ru - sa - lem, Christ is born in Beth-le-hem.
ALL VOICES
f
6. Teach, O teach us, Ho - ly Child, By thy face so
ORGAN
f
Man.
Ped.
meek and mild, Teach us to re - sem - ble thee, In thy sweet hu - mi - li - ty:

CHOIR I (and audience)
Hail, thou e - ver - bless-ed morn; Hail, re-demp-tion's hap-py dawn;
CHOIR II
Hail, thou e - ver - bless-ed morn; Hail, re-demp-tion's hap-py dawn;
ORGAN
Largamente
Sing through all Je - ru - sa-lem, Christ is born in Beth - le - hem.
Largamente
Sing through all Je - ru - sa - lem, Christ is born in Beth - le - hem.
Largamente

34. LUTE-BOOK LULLABY

Words by
W. BALLET

W. BALLET (17th c.)
arranged by GEOFFREY SHAW

Reprinted from *The Oxford Book of Carols* by permission

lul - la, lul - la - by. 2. 'Sweet babe,' sang she, 'my
son, And eke a sa - viour born, Who hast vouch-
-saf - ed from on high To vis - it us that were for-
To vis - it us, us that were for-
- lorn: La-lu - la, la - lu - la, la - lu - la - by. Sweet babe,' sang
- lorn: La-lu - la, la - lu - la, la - lu - la - by. Sweet babe,' sang
she, And rocked him sweet - - - ly on her knee.

From the MS. *Lute Book* by William Ballet, early seventeenth century, Trinity College, Dublin.

35. THE LINDEN TREE CAROL

Tr. G. R. WOODWARD

Old German tune
arranged by REGINALD JACQUES

Verses 1, 3, 5
SOPRANO
ALTO
TENOR
BASS
1. There stood in heav'n a lin - - den tree, But, tho' t'was ho - ney - la - - - den, All an - gels cried, 'No bloom shall be Like that of one fair maid - - en.'
3. 'Hail Ma - ry!' quoth the an - - gel mild, 'Of wo - man - kind the fair - - - est: The Vir - gin ay shalt thou be styled, A babe al - though thou bear - - est.'
5. This ti - - ding fill'd his mates with glee: 'Twas pass'd from one to o - - - ther, That 'twas Ma - ry, and none but she, And God would call her Mo - - ther.

Words reprinted from *The Cambridge Carol Book* by permission

Verses 2, 4

SOPRANO
ALTO
TENOR
and
BARITONE
2. Sped_ Ga - bri - el on wing - - ed
4. 'So___ be it!' God's hand - maid - - en

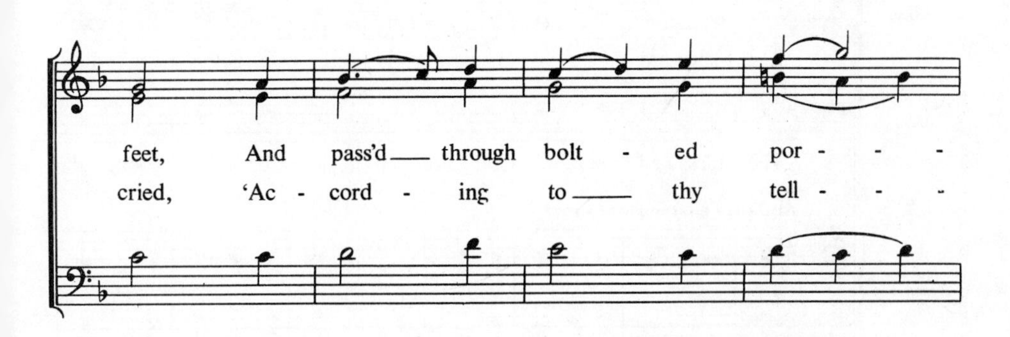
feet, And pass'd___ through bolt - ed por - - -
cried, 'Ac - cord - ing to___ thy tell - - -

-tals In Na - za - reth,___ a maid___ to
-ing.' Where - on___ the an - gel smart - ly

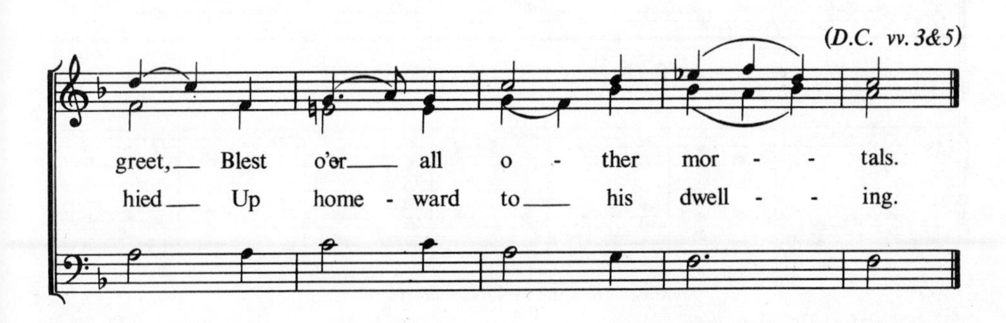
(D.C. vv. 3&5)
greet,___ Blest o'er___ all o - ther mor - - tals.
hied___ Up home - ward to___ his dwell - - ing.

36. THE BLESSED SON OF GOD

Words by
MILES COVERDALE
after MARTIN LUTHER

R. VAUGHAN WILLIAMS

Reprinted from the cantata *Hodie* (O.U.P.)

-last - ing good. Ky-ri-e-lei - - son. Lord have mer - - cy. The
-last - ing good. Ky-ri-e-lei - - son. Lord have mer - - cy. The
-last - ing good. Ky-ri-e-lei - - son. Lord have mer - - cy. The
-last - ing good. Ky-ri-e-lei - - son. Lord have mer - - cy. The
1
Lord Christ Je - su, God's son dear, Was a guest and a strang - er here;
Lord Christ Je - su, God's son dear, Was a guest and a strang - er here;
Lord Christ Je - su, God's son dear, Was a guest and a strang - er here;
Lord Christ Je - su, God's son dear, Was a guest and a strang - er here;
1

Us for to bring from mi - se - ry, That we might live e - ter - nal - ly.
Us for_to bring from mi - se - ry, That we_might live_ e - ter - nal - ly.
Us for_to bring from mi - se - ry, That we might live_ e - ter - nal - ly.
Us for to bring from mi - se - ry,_That we_might live e - ter - nal - ly.
2
pp
Ky - ri - e - lei - son.
Lord_ have mer - cy.
All this did he
p cantabile
All this did he for
p cantabile

ahs
for us free-ly, For to de-clare his great mer-cy; All Christ-en-
for us free-ly, For to de-clare his great mer-cy; All Christ-en-
for us free-ly, For to de-clare his great mer-cy; All Christ-en-
us free-ly, For to de-clare his great mer-cy; All Christ-en-
-dom be mer-ry there-fore, And give him thanks for ev-er-more,
-dom be mer-ry there-fore, And give him thanks for ev-er-more,
-dom be mer-ry there-fore, And give him thanks for ev-er-more,
-dom be mer-ry there-fore, And give him thanks for ev-er-more,

3
p
ev - - - er - more.
Ky - ri - e - lei - - - son,
Lord have mer - - - cy,
ev - er - more.
Ky - ri - e - lei, e - lei - - - son,
Lord have mer - cy, mer - - - cy
Ky - ri - e - lei - son, e - lei - - - son,
Lord have mer - cy, have mer - - - cy,
Ky - ri - e - lei - - - son. Ky - ri - e - lei - - - son,
Lord have mer - - - cy, Lord have mer - - - cy,
pp
Ky - ri - e - lei - - - son.
Lord have mer - - - cy.
Ky - ri - e - lei - - - son.
Lord have mer - - cy, mer - - - cy.
Ky - ri - e - lei - - - son.
Lord have mer - - cy, mer - - - cy.
Ky - ri - e - lei - - son.
Lord have mer - - cy, mer - - - cy.
eh
ih
aw
HEMIOLA

To Cuthbert Bates and the City of Bath Bach Choir, by whom this setting was commissioned.

37. THE BOAR'S HEAD CAROL

English traditional carol
arranged by ELIZABETH POSTON

The tune, and the words of verses 1, 2, and 5, are as sung at Queen's College, Oxford. To provide an optional extension of the Oxford carol, two verses have been incorporated (nos. 3 & 4), fitted to the Oxford tune, from a Boar's Head carol of BM MS Addit. 5665, c. 1500, bearing the signature Smert, and probably from the West Country, where Richard Smert was rector of Plymtree near Exeter, 1435-1477.

(Bass Solo)
boar's head in hand bear I, Be-deck'd with bays and rose - ma - ry. And I
pray you, my mas - ters, be mer - ry, Quot es - tis in con - vi - vi - o.
S.
A.
Ca - put a - pri de - fe - ro, Red - dens lau - des Do - mi - no.
T.
B.
2. The boar's head, as I un - der - stand, Is the brav-est dish in all the
land, When thus be-deck'd with a gay gar - land. Let us ser - vi - re can - ti - co.

*Alternative in small notes in case it be found preferable to reserve high tenor tone for later passages. Altos divide (small notes) if tenors use alternative notes.

subito poco p
Ca - put a - pri — de - fe - ro, — Red-dens lau - des — Do - mi - no.
subito poco p
f
Ca - put a - pri de - fe - ro, Red-dens lau - des Do - mi - no.
f
OPTIONAL SEMI-CHORUS
p
(Now-ell, now-ell, now - ell, now - ell, — now - ell, — now-ell, now-
mp
3. The boar's head that we bring here Be - to-ken-eth a prince with-out - e
p
(Now-ell, now-ell, now - ell, now - ell, — now - ell, — now-ell, now-
p
Now-ell, now-ell, now - ell, now - ell, — now - ell, — now-ell, now-
p

sempre p
-ell), Is born this day to buy us dear; Now-ell, now-ell, now-ell, now-ell.
sempre p
peer Is born this day to buy us dear; Now-ell, now-ell, now-ell.
sempre p
-ell), Is born this day to buy us dear; Now-ell, now-ell, now-ell, now-ell.
mf
-ell), Is born this day to buy us dear; Now-

Now - ell, now - ell, now - ell, now - ell.
Now - ell, now - ell, now - ell, now - ell.
Now - ell, now - ell, now - ell, now - ell.
-ell, now-ell, now-ell, now-ell, Tid-ings good I think to tell.

FULL
Ca - put a - pri de - fe - ro, Red - dens lau - des Do - mi - no.
Ca - put a - pri de - fe ro, Red - dens lau - des Do - mi - no.
Ca - put a - pri de - fe - ro, Red - dens lau - des Do - mi - no.
Ca - put a - pri de - fe - ro, Red - dens lau - des Do - mi - no.
OPTIONAL SEMI-CHORUS
Now - - ell, now - ell,
4. This boar's head we bring with song, Now - ell,
4. This boar's head we bring with song,
Now - ell, In wor - ship

Optional solo
flessible
now - - - - - ell,
now - - - - - - ell. Of a
now - - - - - ell.
Of a
now - - - - ell.
Of a
of him that thus sprang
Of a
Optional solo
Now - ell, now - ell, now - ell.
vir - gin to re - dress all wrong;
Now-
vir - gin to re - dress all wrong;
Now -
vir - gin to re - dress all wrong;
Now -
(9)
vir - gin to re - dress all wrong;
Now -

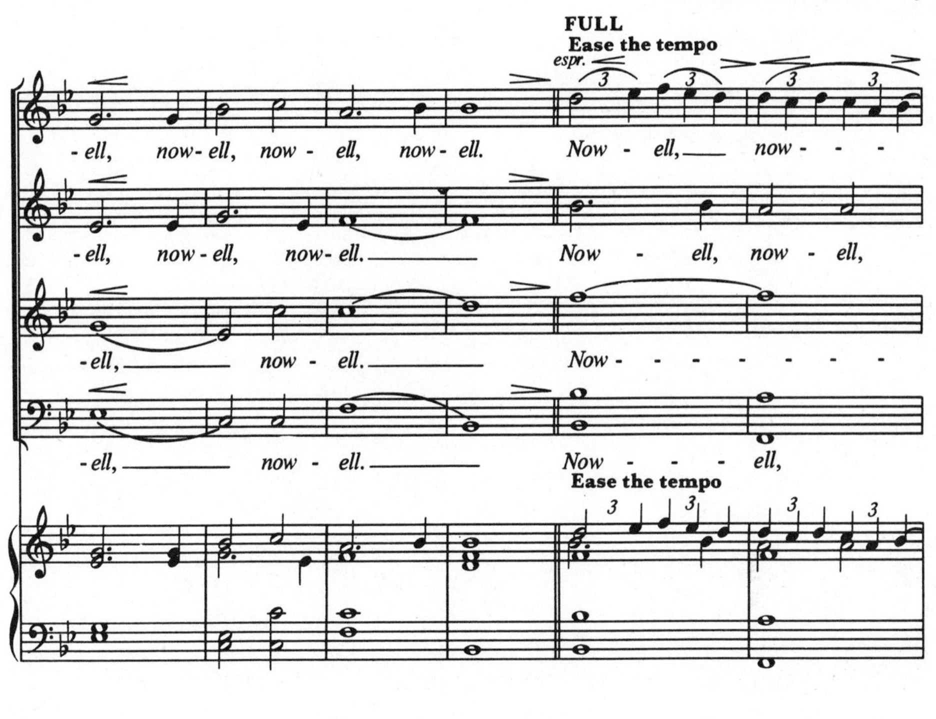
FULL
Ease the tempo
espr.
-ell, now-ell, now-ell, now-ell. Now-ell, now-
-ell, now-ell, now-ell. Now-ell, now-ell,
-ell, now-ell. Now-
-ell, now-ell. Now-ell,
Ease the tempo

rit.
-ell, now-ell, now-ell.
now-ell, Tid-ings good I think to tell.
-ell, now-ell, now-ell.
now-ell, now-ell.
rit.

a tempo
mf
5. Our stew - ard hath pro - vid - ed this In hon - our of the King of
King of
Bliss, Which on this day to be serv - ed is, In Re - gi - nen - si A - tri - o.

Ca - put a - pri de - fe - ro, Red - dens lau - des
Largamente
1
2
Do - mi - no. -no. Now - ell, now - ell.
f
ff

38. THE FIRST NOWELL

English traditional carol
arranged by DAVID WILLCOCKS

VOICES
ORGAN
mf FULL
mf
Man.
Ped.
The_ first ___ No- -well the_ an- gel did say Was to cer- tain poor shep- herds in
fields as they lay; In_ fields_ where they lay,- keep- ing their sheep, On a
cold win- ter's night_ that was__ so deep:
f REFRAIN
f
No - well,___ No - - well, No- well, No - well, Born is the King_ of Is - ra - el!

SOPRANO ALTO
(ORGAN)
TENOR BASS
mf
2. They look - ed up and saw a star, Shining in the east, be - yond them far; And to the earth it gave great light, And so it con - tin - ued both day and night:
4. This star drew nigh to the north-west; O'er Beth - le - hem it took its rest, And there it did both stop and stay Right ov - er the place where Je - sus lay:
REFRAIN (voices in unison)
f
No - well, No - well, No - well, No - well,
Born is the King of Is - ra - el!
ORGAN

Note: vv. 2 & 4 may be sung by unaccompanied voices.

Note: vv. 3 & 5 may be sung unaccompanied, or with organ, or by unison voices (tenor part) with descant (soprano part), and organ.

Tune.

FULL
VOICES
ORGAN
6. Then let us all with one accord Sing praises to our heav'n-ly Lord, That hath made heav'n and earth of naught, And with his blood man-kind hath bought:
REFRAIN
DESCANT (Sops.)
No-well, No-well, No-well, No-well, Born is the King of Is-ra-el!

To the Bach Choir

39. THE HOLLY AND THE IVY

English traditional carol
arranged by REGINALD JACQUES

Moderato
mf
SOPRANO
1. The hol-ly and the i - vy, When they are both full grown, Of
ALTO
1. The hol-ly and the i - vy, When they are both full grown, Of
TENOR
1. The hol-ly and the i - vy, When they are both full grown, Of
BASS
1. The hol-ly and the i - vy, When they are both full grown, Of
(for practice only)
CHORUS
f
all the trees that are in the wood, The holly bears the crown. The

 This carol was collected by Cecil Sharp.

ris- ing of the sun, — And the run-ning of the deer, The—
ris - ing of the— sun, And the run-ning of— the— deer,— The
ris- ing of the sun, And the run-ning of the— deer,— The
ris- ing of the sun, — And the run-ning of— the deer, — The
FINE
play-ing of the mer - ry or - gan, Sweet sing-ing in the choir.
play- ing of the mer - ry or - gan, Sweet sing-ing in— the— choir.
play - ing of the mer - ry or - gan, Sweet sing- ing in the choir.
play-ing of the— mer - ry or - gan, Sweet sing-ing in the choir.
FINE

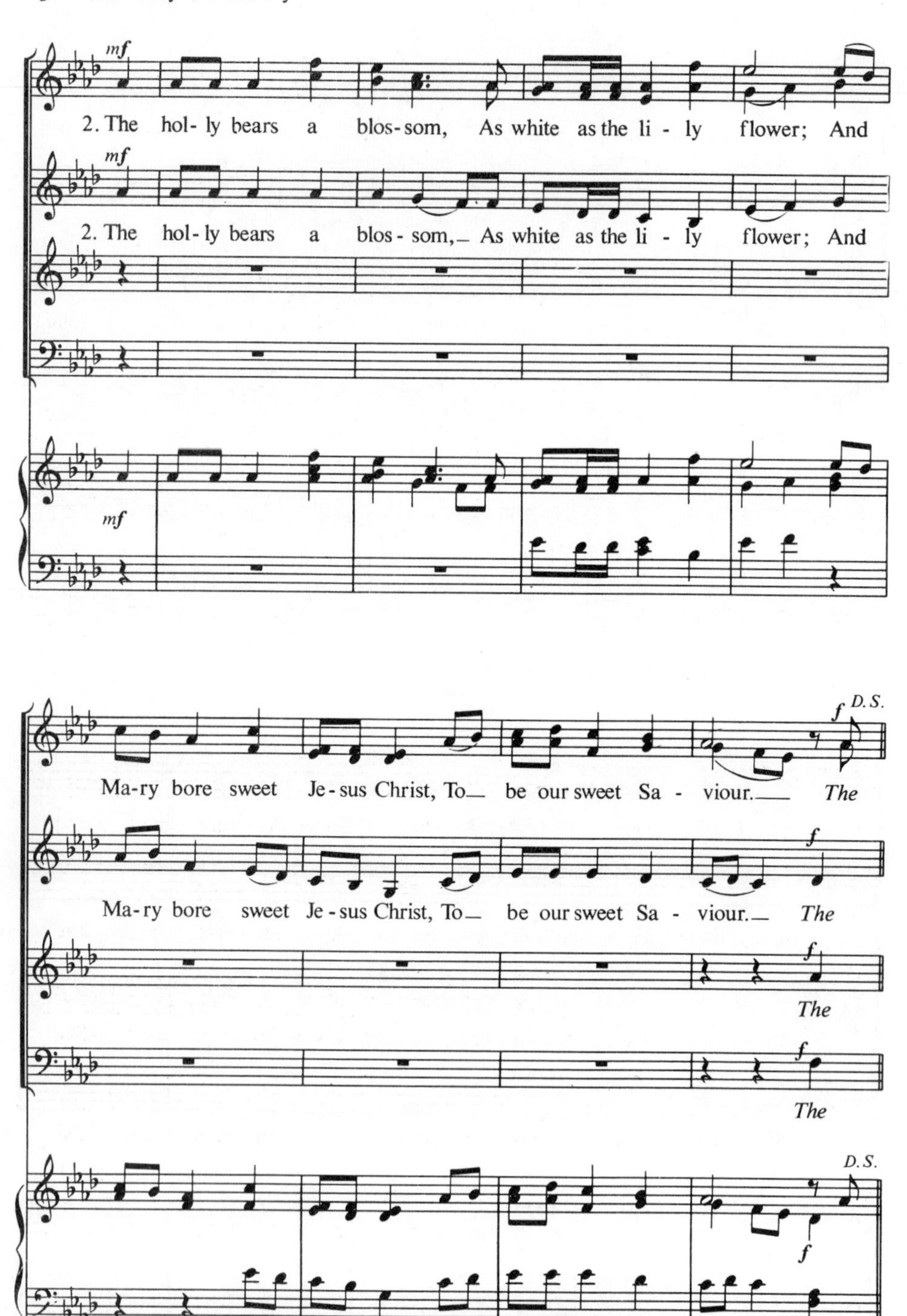
mf
2. The hol-ly bears a blos-som, As white as the li - ly flower; And
mf
2. The hol-ly bears a blos-som, As white as the li - ly flower; And
mf
Ma-ry bore sweet Je-sus Christ, To be our sweet Sa - viour. The
Ma-ry bore sweet Je-sus Christ, To be our sweet Sa - viour. The
f
The
f
The
D.S.
f
D.S.
f

mf
3. The hol-ly bears a ber - ry, As red as a - ny_ blood;_ And
mf
3. The hol-ly bears a_ ber - ry, As_ red as a - ny_ blood; And
mf
And
mf
And
mf

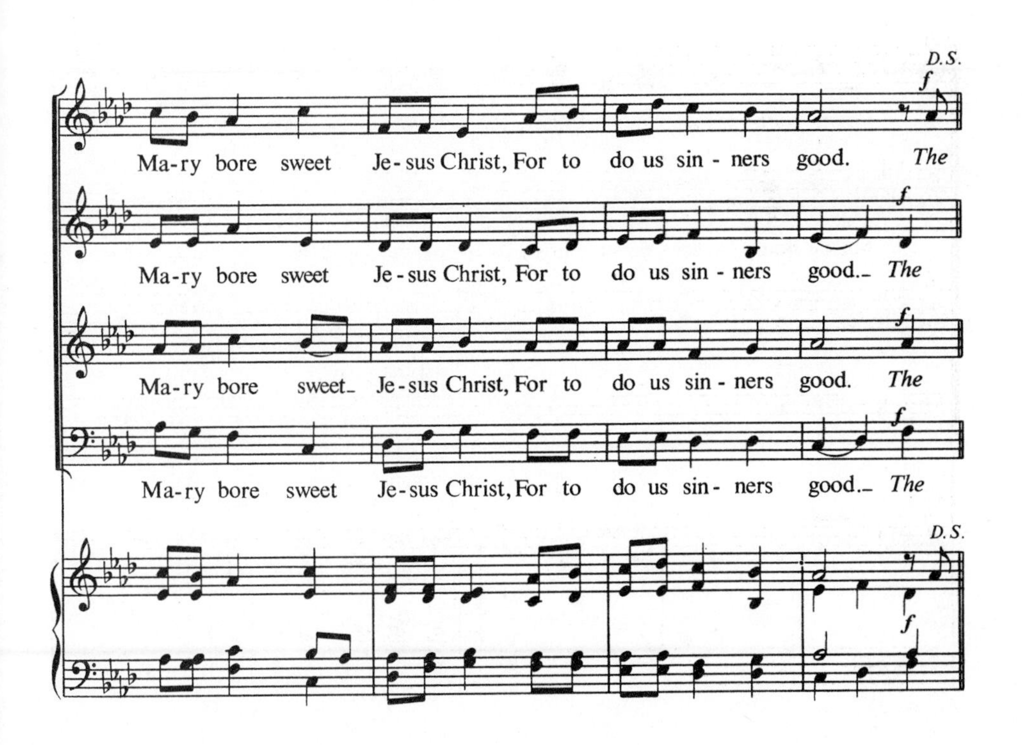
D.S.
f
Ma-ry bore sweet Je-sus Christ, For to do us sin - ners good. The
f
Ma-ry bore sweet Je-sus Christ, For to do us sin - ners good._ The
f
Ma-ry bore sweet_ Je-sus Christ, For to do us sin - ners good. The
f
Ma-ry bore sweet Je-sus Christ, For to do us sin- ners good._ The
D.S.
f

mf
4. The hol-ly bears a pri - ckle, As sharp as a - ny thorn, And
4. The hol-ly bears a pri - ckle, As sharp as a - ny thorn,_ And
And
4. The hol-ly bears a pri - ckle, As sharp as a - ny thorn, And Ma-ry bore sweet
Ma-ry bore sweet Je-sus Christ, On_Christ-mas day in the morn. The
Ma-ry bore sweet Je-sus Christ, On_Christ-mas day in the morn._ The
Ma-ry bore sweet Je-sus Christ, On Christ-mas day in the morn. The
Je - sus On Christ-mas day in the morn._ The
D.S.
f

mf
5. The hol-ly bears a bark, As bit-ter as a-ny gall; And
mf
5. The hol-ly bears a bark, As bit-ter as a-ny gall; And
mf
as a-ny gall; And
mf

D.S.
Ma-ry bore sweet Je-sus Christ, For to re-deem us all. The
Ma-ry bore sweet Je-sus Christ, For to re-deem us all. The
Ma-ry bore sweet Je-sus Christ, For to re-deem us all. The
mf
Ma-ry bore sweet Je-sus Christ, For to re-deem us all. The
f
D.S.

After verse 5 repeat verse 1

40. THE THREE KINGS

Tr. H. N. BATE

PETER CORNELIUS
arranged by IVOR ATKINS

SOLO
SOPRANO
ALTO
TENOR
BASS
(for practice only)
mf
1. Three kings from Per - sian lands a - far To Jor-dan fol - low the
* CHORALE Wie schön leuchtet der Morgenstern
pp well sustained
How bright-ly shines the
pp well sustained
How bright-ly shines the
pp
point - ing star: And this the quest of the tra - vel- lers three, Where the
morn - ing star! With grace and
p
morn - ing star! With grace and
p
p

* The singers should be placed, if possible, at some distance from the soloist.

new-born King of the Jews may_ be. Full roy - al gifts they bear for the
truth from heav'n a - far Our
pp
truth from heav'n a - far Our
pp
pp
King; Gold, in - cense, myrrh are their of - fer - ing. 2. The star shines
Jes - se tree_ now blow - - eth.
Jes - se tree now blow - - eth.

out with a stead-fast ray; The kings to Beth-le-hem
pp
Of Ja-cob's stem and
make their way, And there in wor-ship they bend the knee, As Ma-ry's
Da-vid's line, For thee, my
p
poco

child— in her— lap they— see; Their roy - al gifts they show to the
Bride - groom, King di - vine, My
Bride - groom, King di - vine, My
Bride - groom, King di - vine, My
Bride - groom, King di - vine, My
King; Gold, in - cense, myrrh are their of - fer - ing.— Thou child of man,
soul with love o'er - flow - eth. Thy word,—
soul with love— o'er - flow - eth. Thy word,
soul with love o'er - flow - eth. Thy— word,—
soul with love o'er - flow - eth. Thy word,

lo, to Beth-le-hem The kings are trav'-lling,_ trav-el with them!
— Je - su,
Thy word, Je - su, Je - su,
Thy_ word, Je - su,_ Je - su,
Thy word, Je - su, Je - su,
poco a poco più mosso
The star of mer- cy, the star of grace, Shall lead thy_heart to its rest - ing -
In - ly feeds us, Right - ly leads us,
In - ly feeds us,_ Right - ly leads us,_
In - ly feeds us,_ Right - ly leads us,_
In - ly feeds us, Right - ly leads us,

-place. Gold, in-cense, myrrh thou canst not bring; Of-fer thy heart to the
Life be-stow - - - ing. Praise, O
Life be - stow - - ing. Praise, O praise, praise, O
Life be - stow - - ing. Praise, O
Life be - stow - - ing. Praise, O
f
in - fant King, Of - fer thy heart!
praise such love o'er - flow - - ing.
praise such love o'er - flow - - ing.
praise such love o'er - flow - - ing.
praise such love o'er - flow - - ing.
pp

41. THE SHEPHERDS' FAREWELL

(FROM 'L'ENFANCE DU CHRIST' Op.25)

Words by PAUL ENGLAND

HECTOR BERLIOZ

* Here, and elsewhere, alternative notes (small) are provided for basses.

p
-tent our earth-ly lot to share, Lov-ing fa-ther, lov-ing mo-ther.
p
- - tent our earth-ly lot to share, Lov-ing fa-ther, lov-ing mo-ther,
p
-tent our earth-ly lot to share, Lov-ing fa-ther, lov-ing mo-ther,
p
-tent our earth-ly lot to share, Fa - ther, lov-ing mo-ther,
p
f mf dim.
Shel-ter thee with ten-der care! Lov-ing fa-ther, lov-ing mo-ther,
f mf dim.
Shel-ter thee with ten-der care! Lov-ing fa-ther, lov-ing mo-ther,
f mf dim.
Shel-ter thee with ten-der care! Lov-ing fa-ther, lov-ing mo-ther,
f mf dim.
Shel-ter thee with ten-der care! Lov-ing fa-ther, lov-ing mo-ther.
f mf dim.

poco rit.
p
Shel - ter thee with ten - der care, shel - ter thee with ten - der care!
Shel - ter thee with ten - der care, shel - ter thee with ten - der care!
Shel- ter thee with ten - der care, shel - ter thee with ten - der care!
Shel- ter thee with ten - der care, shel - ter thee with ten - der care!
Tempo I
Bless - ed Je - sus, we im-plore thee With
Oboes
f Clar.
Strings

poco f
hum - ble love and ho - ly fear, In the land that lies_ be - fore thee, For -
poco f
hum - ble love and ho - ly fear, In the land that_lies be - fore thee, For-
poco f
hum - ble love and ho - ly fear, In the land that lies be - fore thee, For-
poco f
hum - ble love and ho - ly fear, In the land that lies be-fore thee, For-
poco f
p
- get not us who lin - ger here! May the shep-herd's low - ly call - ing,
p
- - get not_ us who lin - ger here! May the shep-herd's low - ly call - ing,
p
- get not us who lin - ger here! May the shepherd's low-ly call - ing,
p
-get_ not us_who lin-ger here! May the shepherd's low-ly call - ing,
p

mf
dim.
f
Ev - er to thy heart be dear! May the shep-herd's low - ly call - ing,
Ev-er to thy heart be dear! May the shep-herd's low - ly call - ing,
Ev-er to thy heart be dear! May the shep-herd's low - ly call - ing,
Ev - er to thy heart be dear! May the shep - herd's low - ly call - ing,
poco rit.
p
Ev - er to thy heart be dear, ev - er to thy heart be dear!
Ev - er to thy heart be dear, ev - er to thy heart be dear!
Ev-er to thy heart be dear, ev - er to thy heart be dear!
Ev - er to thy heart be dear, ev - er to thy heart be dear!

Tempo I
Un poco più lento
pppp
Blest are ye be-yond all measure, Thou hap-py
Blest are ye be-yond all measure, Thou hap-py
Blest are ye be-yond all measure, Thou hap-py
Blest are ye be-yond all measure, Thou hap-py
Tempo I
Oboes
f
Clar.
Un poco più lento
Strings
pppp
fa-ther, mo-ther mild! Guard ye well your heav'n-ly trea-sure, The
fa-ther, mo-ther mild! Guard ye well your heav'n-ly trea-sure, The
fa-ther, mo-ther mild! Guard ye well your heav'n-ly trea-sure, The
fa-ther, mo-ther mild! Guard ye well your heav'n-ly trea-sure, The

Prince of Peace, the Ho - ly Child! God go with you, God_ pro-
_Prince of Peace, the Ho - ly Child! God go with you, God pro-
Prince of Peace, the Ho - ly Child! God go with you, God pro-
Prince of Peace, the Ho-ly Child! God go with you, God pro-
-tect_ you, Guide you safe - ly through the wild! God_ go with_ you,
-tect you, Guide you safe - ly through the wild! God go with_ you,
-tect you, Guide you safe - ly through the wild! God go with_ you,
-tect you, Guide you safe - ly through the wild! God go with you,

un poco rit.
God_ pro - tect_ you, Guide you safe - ly through the wild, guide you
un poco rit.
God pro - tect_ you, Guide you safe - ly_ through the wild, guide you
un poco rit.
God pro - tect_ you, Guide you safe - ly through the wild,_ guide you
un poco rit.
God pro-tect you, Guide you safe - ly through the wild,___ guide you
un poco rit.
safe - ly through the wild!
safe - ly through the wild!
safe - ly through the wild!
safe - ly through the wild!
Oboes
pp Clar.

42. TORCHES

Tr. J. B. TREND
(from the Galician)

JOHN JOUBERT

Alla marcia
mf
VOICES
ORGAN
mf
simile
Ped.
1. Tor-ches, tor-ches, run_with_tor-ches All_ the_ way to_
Beth-le-hem! Christ is born and now_ lies_ sleep-ing; Come_ and_ sing your_
song to him! Tor-ches, tor-ches, run_ with_ tor-ches All_ the_ way to_
Beth-le-hem! Christ is born and now_lies_ sleep-ing; Come_and_sing your_ song to him!

Words from *The Oxford Book of Carols* by permission
Music reprinted by permission of Novello & Co. Ltd.

SOPRANO
ALTO
TENOR
BASS
p
Ah, Ro-ro, Ro-ro, my baby, Ah, Ro-ro, my love, Ro-ro;
Ro - ro, Ro - ro,
Ro - ro, Ro - ro,
Ro - ro, Ro - ro,
p unaccompanied ad lib.
Man.

Sleep you well, my heart's own darling, While we sing you our Ro-ro.
Ro - - ro, Ro - ro, sing Ro - ro.
Ro - - ro, Ro - ro, sing Ro - ro.
Ro - - ro, Ro - ro, sing Ro - ro.

f
Sing, my friends, and make– you– mer - ry, Joy– and– mirth and–
f
Sing, my friends, and make you mer - ry,
f
Sing, my friends, and make– you– mer - ry, Joy– and– mirth and–
f
Sing, my friends, and make you mer - ry,
f
Ped.
joy a - gain; Lo, he lives, the King– of– hea - ven, Now– and– ev - er-
Sing, my friends, and make you mer - ry, Sing my friends,– Now and ev - er-
joy a - gain; Lo, he lives, the King– of– hea - ven, Now– and– ev - er-
Sing, my friends, and make you mer - ry, Sing, my friends,– Now and ev - er-

ff
-more. A - men. Lo, he lives, the King of heaven,
-more. A - men. Lo, he lives, the King of heaven,
-more. A - men. Lo, he lives, the King of heaven,
-more. A - men. Lo, he lives, the King of heaven,
allarg.
Now and ev - er, ev - er - more. A - men.
Now and ev - er - more. A - men.
Now and ev - er - more. A - men.
Now and ev - er - more. A - men.
allarg.

43. UNTO US IS BORN A SON

Tr. G. R. WOODWARD

Tune from *Piae Cantiones*, 1582
arranged by DAVID WILLCOCKS

VOICES
ORGAN
FULL
f
1. Un - to us is
Man.
Ped.
born a Son, King of quires su - per - nal: See on earth his
life be - gun, Of lords the Lord e - ter - nal, of lords the Lord e - ter - nal.
S.
* Voices unaccompanied
mf
A.
2. Christ, from heav'n des - cend - ing low, Comes on earth a stran - ger; Ox and ass their
T.
B.
mf

*may be sung accompanied, or by unison voices and organ
Words reprinted from *The Cowley Carol Book* by permission

own - er know, Be- cra-dled in the_ man - ger, be - cra-dled in the man - ger.
TENORS and BASSES
f
3. This did He-rod sore af - fray, And grie-vous - ly be - wild - er, So he gave the
mf
Full Sw.
f
Ped.
Man.
word to slay, And slew the lit - tle chil - der, and slew the lit - tle chil - der.
f
ff
Ped.
SOPRANOS
mp
4. Of his love and mer - cy mild This the Christ-mas sto - ry; And O that Ma - ry's
p
Man.
gen - tle Child Might lead us up to glo - ry, might lead us up to glo - ry!

Ist Choir
UNISON VOICES
f
ff
5. O and A, and A and O, Cum cant-i-bus in cho - ro, Let our mer-ry
*2nd Choir
SOPRANO ALTO
f
ff
5. O and A, and A and O, Cum cant-i-bus in cho - ro, Let our mer-ry
TENOR BASS
f
ff
ORGAN
f
ff
Man.
Ped.

or- gan go, Be - ne- di- ca-mus Do-mi- no, be - ne- di- ca- mus Do - mi-no.
or- gan go, Be - ne- di- ca-mus Do-mi - no, be - ne - di - ca-mus Do-mi - no.

*optional, or soprano part as a descant.

44. UP! GOOD CHRISTEN FOLK, AND LISTEN

Words by G. R. WOODWARD

Tune from *Piae Cantiones*, 1582
harmonized by G. R. WOODWARD

SOPRANO
ALTO
TENOR
BASS
Ding-dong, ding: Ding-a-dong-a-ding: Ding-dong, ding-dong: Ding-a-dong-ding.
Up! good Christen folk, and list-en_ How the mer-ry church - bells ring,
Tell the sto-ry how from glo-ry_ God came down at Christ - mas-tide,
And from stee-ple_ bid good peo-ple Come a-dore the new - born_ King:
Bring-ing glad-ness,_ cha-sing sad-ness, Show'ring blessings far_ and_ wide,
Born of_ mo-ther, blest o'er o-ther, Ex Ma-ri-a Vir-gi-ne,
In a sta-ble ('tis no fa-ble), Chris-tus na-tus ho - di - e.

Reprinted from *The Cowley Carol Book* by permission

45. WE'VE BEEN AWHILE A-WANDERING

Traditional Yorkshire carol
collected and arranged by
R. VAUGHAN WILLIAMS

Allegro
VOICES
PIANO or ORGAN
pp
1. We've been a-while a-wan-der-ing A-mongst the leaves so green,— But now we come a-was-sail-ing, So plain-ly to be seen; For it's Christmas time, when we tra-vel far and near; May God
2. We are not dai-ly beg-gars That beg from door to door;— We are your neigh-bours' child-ren, For we've been here be-fore;
v.3
v.5
The accompaniment may be performed by voices ('Ah' or humming)

Reprinted from *Eight Traditional Carols* by permission of Stainer & Bell. Ltd.

bless you and send you a hap-py New Year.
rall.

3. We've got a little purse,
Made of leathern ratchin skin;
We want a little of your money
To line it well within;
For it's, etc.

4. Call up the butler of this house,
Likewise the mistress too,
And all the little children
That round the table go;
For it's, etc.

(♩ ♪)
5. Bring us out a table
And spread it with a cloth,
Bring us out a mouldy cheese
And some of your Christmas loaf;
For it's, etc.

6. Good master and good mistress,
While you're sitting by the fire,
Pray think of us poor children
That's wandered in the mire;
For it's, etc.

46. GLOUCESTERSHIRE WASSAIL

English traditional carol
arranged by R. VAUGHAN WILLIAMS

In quick time
SOPRANO
ALTO
TENOR
BASS
1. Was - sail, was - sail, all o - ver the town! Our
2. So here is to Cher-ry and to his right cheek, Pray
toast it is white, and our ale it is brown, Our
God send our mas - ter a good piece of beef, And a
bowl it is made of the white ma - ple tree; With the
good piece of beef that may we all see; With the
was - sail - ing bowl we'll drink to thee.
was - sail - ing bowl we'll drink to thee.

Reprinted from *The Oxford Book of Carols* by permission

3. And here is to Dobbin and to his right eye,
Pray God send our master a good Christmas pie,
And a good Christmas pie that may we all see;
With our wassailing bowl we'll drink to thee.

4. So here is to Broad May and to her broad horn,
May God send our master a good crop of corn,
And a good crop of corn that may we all see;
With the wassailing bowl we'll drink to thee.

5. And here is to Fillpail and to her left ear,
Pray God send our master a happy New Year,
And a happy New Year as e'er he did see;
With our wassailing bowl we'll drink to thee.

6. And here is to Colly and to her long tail,
Pray God send our master he never may fail
A bowl of strong beer; I pray you draw near,
And our jolly wassail it's then you shall hear.

7. Come, butler, come fill us a bowl of the best,
Then we|hope that your|soul in|heaven may|rest;
But|if you do draw us a bowl of the small,
Then down shall go butler, bowl and all.

8. Then here's to the maid in the lily white smock,
Who tripped to the door and slipped back the lock!
Who tripped to the door and pulled back the pin,
For to let these jolly wassailers in.

Wassail, Wes hal, Old English, 'Be thou whole' (hale); a form of salutation, and hence a festive occasion. Cf. 'wassail bowl', cup, or horn.

Cherry and Dobbin are horses. Broad May, Fillpail, and Colly are cows.

47. WHAT CHEER?

Words from RICHARD HILL'S Commonplace Book (16th. c.)

WILLIAM WALTON

SOPRANO
ALTO
TENOR
BASS
Allegretto
marcato
p
fz
cresc.
What cheer? Good cheer! Be
What cheer? Good cheer!
mer - ry and glad this good New Year!
f
'Lift up your hearts and be glad In Christ's birth', the
an - gel bade, Say each to o - ther, if a - ny be
sad: 'What cheer? What cheer? What cheer? What cheer?'
'What cheer?'

p
Now the King of heav'n his birth hath take,
p
Joy and mirth we ought to make; Say each to
o - ther, for his sake: 'What cheer? What
'What cheer?'
cheer? What cheer? What cheer?'
f
I tell you
f
all with heart so free: Right wel - come, wel - come,

ye be to me; Be glad and mer - ry, for cha - ri -
- ty! What cheer? What cheer? Good cheer! Good cheer! Be
What cheer? What cheer? Good cheer! Good cheer! Be

mer - ry and glad, be mer - ry and glad, be

Allargando
mer - ry and glad this good New Year!

48. WHEN CHRIST WAS BORN

Words anon. (15th. c.)

REGINALD JACQUES

Words reprinted from *The Oxford Book of Carols* by permission

49. WHILE SHEPHERDS WATCHED THEIR FLOCKS

Words by
NAHUM TATE (1652-1715)

Este's Psalter, 1592

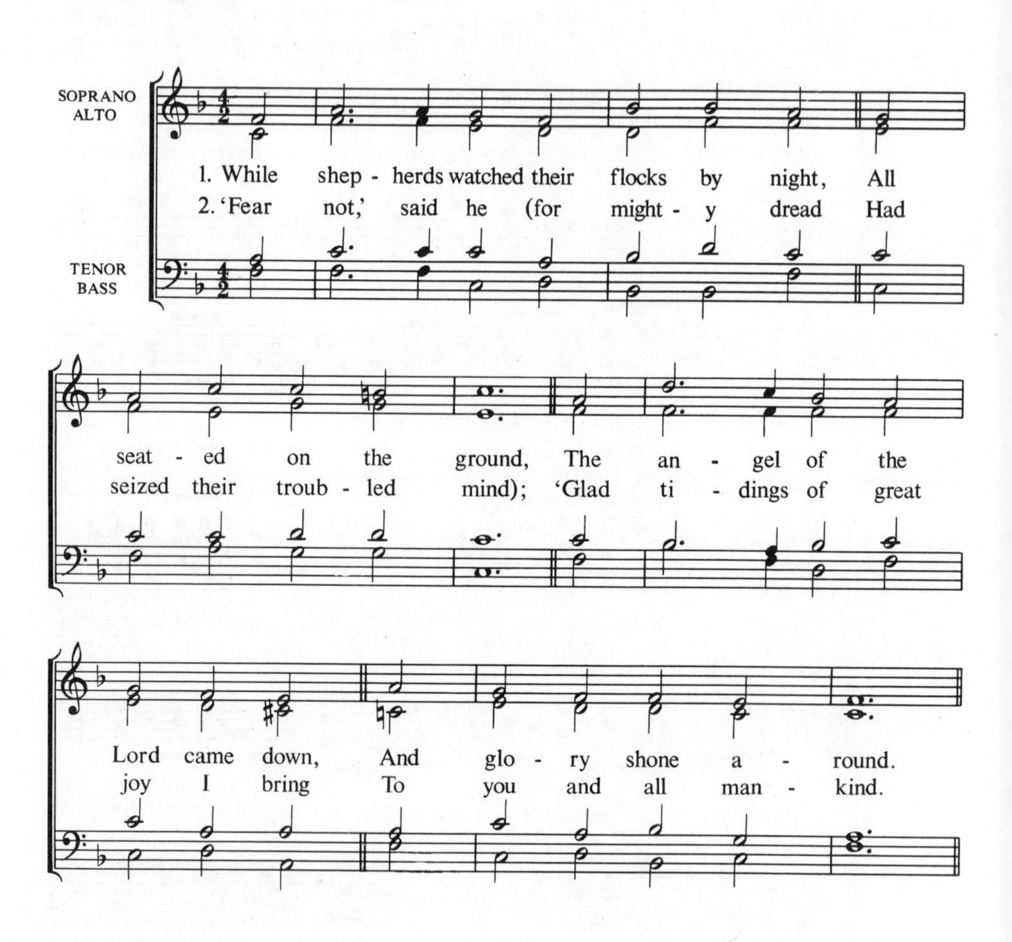
SOPRANO
ALTO
TENOR
BASS
1. While shep - herds watched their flocks by night, All
2. 'Fear not,' said he (for might - y dread Had
seat - ed on the ground, The an - gel of the
seized their troub - led mind); 'Glad ti - dings of great
Lord came down, And glo - ry shone a - round.
joy I bring To you and all man - kind.

3. 'To you in David's town this day
Is born of David's line
A Saviour, who is Christ the Lord;
And this shall be the sign:

4. 'The heavenly Babe you there shall find
To human view displayed,
All meanly wrapped in swathing bands,
And in a manger laid.'

5. Thus spake the Seraph; and forthwith
Appeared a shining throng
Of angels praising God, who thus
Addressed their joyful song:

6. 'All glory be to God on high,
And on the earth be peace;
Good-will henceforth from heaven to men
Begin and never cease.'

ALTERNATIVE VERSION

harmonized by T. RAVENSCROFT (1621)

It is suggested that this version be used for some verses, either by the choir alone, or with the people singing the melody. The tenor part, which has the melody, should be made prominent.

50. WHILE THE SHEPHERDS WERE WATCHING

Words by
BENEDICT ELLIS

C. ARMSTRONG GIBBS

From *A Saviour Born*, a cantata for women's voices (*O.U.P.*)
This carol in its original form (S.S.A.) is also available in the O.C.S. Series (W 13)

sheep, An an - gel came to them and woke them from sleep, His
-vealed, But to rough-and-tum-ble shepherds who were out in the field, Who
sheep, An an - gel came to them and woke them from sleep, His
-vealed, But to rough-and-tum-ble shepherds who were out in the field, Who
sheep, An an - gel came to them and woke them from sleep, His
-vealed, But to rough-and-tum-ble shepherds who were out in the field, Who
sheep, An an - gel came to them and woke them from sleep, His
-vealed, But to rough-and-tum-ble shepherds who were out in the field, Who
mes - sage was sim - ple, as sim - ple as they, But oh, what good
hud - dled in sheep-skins o - ver fires of bleak thorn, Un - til they were
mes - sage was sim - ple, as sim - ple as they, But oh, what good
hud - dled in sheep-skins o - ver fires of bleak thorn, Un - til they were
mes - sage was sim - ple, as sim - ple as they, But oh, what good
hud - dled in sheep-skins o - ver fires of bleak thorn, Un - til they were
mes - sage was sim - ple, as sim - ple as they, But oh, what good
hud - dled in sheep-skins o - ver fires of bleak thorn, Un - til they were

ff
ti - dings he gave_ them that day. Now sing Glo - ry to God, good -
told_ God's_ Son_ had been born.
ff
ti - dings he gave them that day. Now sing Glo - ry to God, good -
told God's_ Son had been born.
ff
ti - dings he gave them that day. Now sing Glo - ry to God, good -
told_ God's_ Son had been born.
ff
ti - dings he gave_ them that day. Now sing Glo - ry to God, good -
told God's_ Son_ had been born.
ff
-will to - wards men, And peace to you all on the earth. A - men.
-will to - wards men,_ And peace to you all on the earth. A - men.
-will to - wards men,_ And peace to you all on the earth. A - men.
-will to - wards men, And_ peace to you all_ on the earth. A - men.

p
Ah
Ah
p
Ah
Ah
SOLI mp
3. Not in a bright pa - lace was young Je - sus found, But
p
Ah
Ah
p
Ah
Ah
Ah
in a dim sta - ble with straw on the ground, His cra - dle a
Ah

Ah
Ah
man - ger, and Ma-ry's soft_ breast Was the gen - tle warm pil - low where
Ah
ff
Now sing Glo - ry to God, good - will to - wards
ff
Now sing Glo - ry to God, good - will to - wards_
he_ took his rest. Now sing Glo - ry to God,_ good - will to - wards_
ff
Now sing Glo - ry to God, good - will to - wards
ff

men, And peace to you all on the earth. A - men.
men, And peace to you all on the earth. A - men.
men, And peace to you all on the earth. A - men.
men, And peace to you all on the earth. A - men.
mf
To these sim-ple shep-herds, to the thief on the tree God
To these sim-ple shep-herds, to the thief on the tree God
To these sim-ple shep-herds, to the thief on the tree God
To these sim-ple shep-herds, to the thief on the tree God

spoke in his mer-cy and he set us all free; And his was the
spoke in his mer-cy and he set us all free; And his was the
spoke in his mer-cy and he set us all free; And his was the
spoke in his mer-cy and he set us all free; And his was the
f
ca - rol, the day Christ was born, That rang from a night-sky as
ca - rol, the day Christ was born, That rang from a night - sky as
ca - rol, the day Christ was born, That rang from a night - sky as
ca - rol, the day Christ was born, That rang from a night - sky as

*Optional line for a few high sopranos

THE NINE LESSONS

The Congregation, standing, shall be bidden to Prayer in these words:

BELOVED in Christ, at this Christmas-tide let it be our care and delight to hear again the message of the angels, and in heart and mind to go even unto Bethlehem and see this thing which is come to pass, and the Babe lying in a manger.

Therefore let us read and mark in Holy Scripture the tale of the loving purposes of God from the first days of our disobedience unto the glorious Redemption brought us by this Holy Child.

But first, let us pray for the needs of the whole world; for peace on earth and goodwill among all his people; for unity and brotherhood within the Church he came to build, and especially in this our diocese.

And because this would rejoice his heart, let us remember, in his name, the poor and helpless, the cold, the hungry, and the oppressed; the sick and them that mourn, the lonely and the unloved, the aged and the little children; all those who know not the Lord Jesus, or who love him not, or who by sin have grieved his heart of love.

Lastly, let us remember before God all those who rejoice with us, but upon another shore, and in a greater light, that multitude which no man can number, whose hope was in the Word made flesh, and with whom in the Lord Jesus we are one for evermore.

These prayers and praises let us humbly offer up to the Throne of Heaven, in the words which Christ himself hath taught us:

OUR Father, which art in heaven, Hallowed be thy name; Thy kingdom come; Thy will be done; In earth as it is in heaven. Give us this day our daily bread. And forgive us our trespasses, As we forgive them that trespass against us. And lead us not into temptation; But deliver us from evil: For thine is the kingdom, The power, and the glory, For ever and ever. Amen.

Then shall the Congregation sit.
The Readers of the Lessons should be appointed after a definite order; in a Cathedral, for instance, from a Chorister up to a Bishop.
Each Reader should proceed to the Reading Desk at the beginning of the last verse of the preceding carol; and announce his Lesson by the descriptive sentence attached to it. At the end of the Lesson, the Reader should pause and say: Thanks be to God.

FIRST LESSON

God announces in the Garden of Eden that the seed of woman shall bruise the serpent's head.

GENESIS iii

AND they heard the voice of the Lord God walking in the garden in the cool of the day: and Adam and his wife hid themselves from the presence of the Lord God amongst the trees of the garden. And the Lord God called unto Adam, and said unto him, Where art thou? And he said, I heard thy voice in the garden, and I was afraid, because I was naked; and I hid myself. And he said, Who told thee that thou wast naked? Hast thou eaten of the tree, whereof I commanded thee that thou shouldest not eat? And the man said, The woman whom thou gavest to be with me, she gave me of the tree, and I did eat. And the Lord God said unto the woman, What is this that thou hast done? And the woman said, The serpent beguiled me, and I did eat. And the Lord God said unto the serpent, Because thou hast done this, thou art cursed above all cattle, and above every beast of the field; upon thy belly shalt thou go, and dust shalt thou eat all the days of thy life: and I will put enmity between thee and the woman, and between thy seed and her seed; it shall bruise thy head, and thou shalt bruise his heel.

SECOND LESSON

God promises to faithful Abraham that in his seed shall the nations of the earth be blessed.

GENESIS xxii

AND the angel of the Lord called unto Abraham out of heaven the second time, and said, By myself have I sworn, saith the Lord, for because thou hast done this thing, and hast not withheld thy son, thine only son: that in blessing I will bless thee, and in multiplying I will multiply thy seed as the stars of the heaven, and as the sand which is upon the sea shore; and thy seed shall possess the gate of his enemies; and in thy seed shall all the nations of the earth be blessed; because thou hast obeyed my voice.

THIRD LESSON

Christ's birth and kingdom are foretold by Isaiah.

ISAIAH ix

THE people that walked in darkness have seen a great light: they that dwell in the land of the shadow of death, upon them hath the light shined. For unto us a child is born, unto us a son is given: and the government shall be upon his shoulder: and his name shall be called Wonderful, Counsellor, the mighty God, the everlasting Father, the Prince of Peace. Of the increase of his government and peace there shall be no end, upon the throne of David, and upon his kingdom, to order it, and to establish it with judgment and with justice from henceforth even for ever. The zeal of the Lord of hosts will perform this.

FOURTH LESSON

The peace that Christ will bring is foreshown.

ISAIAH xi

AND there shall come forth a rod out of the stem of Jesse, and a branch shall grow out of his roots: and the spirit of the Lord shall rest upon him, the spirit of wisdom and understanding, the spirit of counsel and might, the spirit of knowledge and of the fear of the Lord; and shall make him of quick understanding in the fear of the Lord. With righteousness shall he judge the poor, and reprove with equity for the meek of the earth. The wolf also shall dwell with the lamb, and the leopard shall lie down with the kid; and the calf and the young lion and the fatling together; and a little child shall lead them. And the cow and the bear shall feed; their young ones shall lie down together: and the lion shall eat straw like the ox. And the sucking child shall play on the hole of the asp, and the weaned child shall put his hand on the cockatrice' den. They shall not hurt nor destroy in all my holy mountain: for the earth shall be full of the knowledge of the Lord, as the waters cover the sea.

ALTERNATIVE FOURTH LESSON

The prophet Micah foretells the glory of little Bethlehem.

MICAH v

BUT thou, Beth-lehem Ephratah, though thou be little among the thousands of Judah, yet out of thee shall he come forth unto me that is to be ruler in Israel; whose goings forth have been from of old, from everlasting. Therefore will he give them up, until the time that she which travaileth hath brought forth: then the remnant of his brethren shall return unto the children of Israel. And he shall stand and feed in the strength of the Lord, in the majesty of the name of the Lord his God; and they shall abide: for now shall he be great unto the ends of the earth.

FIFTH LESSON

The angel Gabriel salutes the Blessed Virgin Mary.

ST LUKE i

AND in the sixth month the angel Gabriel was sent from God unto a city of Galilee, named Nazareth, to a virgin espoused to a man whose name was Joseph, of the house of David; and the virgin's name was Mary. And the angel came in unto her, and said, Hail, thou that art highly favoured, the Lord is with thee: blessed art thou among women. And when she saw him, she was troubled at his saying, and cast in her mind what manner of salutation this should be. And the angel said unto her, Fear not, Mary: for thou hast found favour with God. And, behold, thou shalt conceive in thy womb, and bring forth a son, and shalt call his name JESUS. He shall be great, and shall be called the Son of the Highest: and the Lord God shall give unto him the throne of his father David: and he shall reign over the house of Jacob for ever; and of his kingdom there shall be no end. Then said Mary unto the angel, How shall this be, seeing I know not a man? And the angel answered and said unto her, The Holy Ghost shall come upon thee, and the power of the Highest shall overshadow thee: therefore also that holy thing which shall be born of thee shall be called the Son of God. And Mary said, Behold the handmaid of the Lord; be it unto me according to thy word. And the angel departed from her.

Alternative fifth lesson – see overleaf

ALTERNATIVE FIFTH LESSON

The prophet in exile foresees the coming of the glory of the Lord.

ISAIAH LX

ARISE, shine; for thy light is come, and the glory of the Lord is risen upon thee. For, behold, the darkness shall cover the earth, and gross darkness the people: but the Lord shall arise upon thee, and his glory shall be seen upon thee. And the Gentiles shall come to thy light, and kings to the brightness of thy rising. Lift up thine eyes round about, and see: all they gather themselves together, they come to thee: thy sons shall come from far, and thy daughters shall be nursed at thy side. Then thou shalt see, and flow together, and thine heart shall fear, and be enlarged; because the abundance of the sea shall be converted unto thee, the forces of the Gentiles shall come unto thee. The multitude of camels shall cover thee, the dromedaries of Midian and Ephah; all they from Sheba shall come: they shall bring gold and incense; and they shall shew forth the praises of the Lord. The sun shall be no more thy light by day; neither for brightness shall the moon give light unto thee: but the Lord shall be unto thee an everlasting light, and thy God thy glory.

SIXTH LESSON

St Matthew tells of the birth of Jesus.

ST MATTHEW i

NOW the birth of Jesus Christ was on this wise: When as his mother Mary was espoused to Joseph, before they came together, she was found with child of the Holy Ghost. Then Joseph her husband, being a just man, and not willing to make her a publick example, was minded to put her away privily. But while he thought on these things, behold, the angel of the Lord appeared unto him in a dream, saying, Joseph, thou son of David, fear not to take unto thee Mary thy wife: for that which is conceived in her is of the Holy Ghost. And she shall bring forth a son, and thou shalt call his name JESUS: for he shall save his people from their sins. Now all this was done, that it might be fulfilled which was spoken of the Lord by the prophet, saying, Behold, a virgin shall be with child, and shall bring forth a son, and they shall call his name Emmanuel, which being interpreted is, God with us.

ALTERNATIVE SIXTH LESSON

St Luke tells of the birth of Jesus.

ST LUKE ii

AND it came to pass in those days, that there went out a decree from Cæsar Augustus, that all the world should be taxed. And all went to be taxed, every one into his own city. And Joseph also went up from Galilee, out of the city of Nazareth, into Judæa, unto the city of David, which is called Bethlehem; (because he was of the house and lineage of David:) to be taxed with Mary his espoused wife, being great with child. And so it was, that, while they were there, the days were accomplished that she should be delivered. And she brought forth her firstborn son, and wrapped him in swaddling clothes, and laid him in a manger; because there was no room for them in the inn.

SEVENTH LESSON

The shepherds go to the manger.

ST LUKE ii

AND there were in the same country shepherds abiding in the field, keeping watch over their flock by night. And, lo, the angel of the Lord came upon them, and the glory of the Lord shone round about them: and they were sore afraid. And the angel said unto them, Fear not: for, behold, I bring you good tidings of great joy, which shall be to all people. For unto you is born this day in the city of David a Saviour, which is Christ the Lord. And this shall be a sign unto you; Ye shall find the babe wrapped in swaddling clothes, lying in a manger. And suddenly there was with the angel a multitude of the heavenly host praising God, and saying, Glory to God in the highest, and on earth peace, good will toward men. And it came to pass, as the angels were gone away from them into heaven, the shepherds said one to another, Let us now go even unto Bethlehem, and see this thing which is come to pass, which the Lord hath made known unto us. And they came with haste, and found Mary, and Joseph, and the babe lying in a manger.

EIGHTH LESSON

The wise men are led by the star to Jesus.

ST MATTHEW ii

NOW when Jesus was born in Bethlehem of Judæa in the days of Herod the king, behold, there came wise men from the east to Jerusalem, saying, Where is he that is born King of the Jews? for we have seen his star in the east, and are come to worship him. When Herod the king had heard these things, he was troubled, and all Jerusalem with him. And when he had gathered all the chief priests and scribes of the people together, he demanded of them where Christ should be born. And they said unto him, In Bethlehem of Judæa: for thus it is written by the prophet, And thou Bethlehem in the land of Juda, art not the least among the princes of Juda: for out of thee shall come a Governor, that shall rule my people Israel. Then Herod, when he had privily called the wise men, inquired of them diligently what time the star appeared. And he sent them to Bethlehem, and said, Go and search diligently for the young child; and when ye have found him, bring me word again, that I may come and worship him also. When they had heard the king, they departed; and lo, the star, which they saw in the east, went before them, till it came and stood over where the young child was. When they saw the star, they rejoiced with exceeding great joy. And when they were come into the house, they saw the young child with Mary his mother, and fell down, and worshipped him: and when they had opened their treasures, they presented unto him gifts, gold, and frankincense, and myrrh.

The Congregation shall stand for the ninth lesson.

NINTH LESSON

St John unfolds the great mystery of the Incarnation.

ST JOHN i

IN the beginning was the Word, and the Word was with God, and the Word was God. The same was in the beginning with God. All things were made by him; and without him was not any thing made that was made. In him was life; and the life was the light of men. And the light shineth in darkness; and the darkness comprehended it not. There was a man sent from God, whose name was John. The same came for a witness, to bear witness of the light, that all men through him might believe. He was not that light, but was sent to bear witness of that light. That was the true light, which lighteth every man that cometh into the world. He was in the world, and the world was made by him, and the world knew him not. He came unto his own, and his own received him not. But as many as received him, to them gave he power to become the sons of God, even to them that believe on his name: which were born, not of blood, nor of the will of the flesh, nor of the will of man, but of God. And the Word was made flesh, and dwelt among us, (and we beheld his glory, the glory as of the only-begotten of the Father,) full of grace and truth.

Priest. The Lord be with you.
Answer. And with thy spirit.
Priest. Let us pray.

All kneel.

THE COLLECT FOR CHRISTMAS EVE

O GOD, who makest us glad with the yearly remembrance of the birth of thy only Son, Jesus Christ: Grant that as we joyfully receive him for our redeemer, so we may with sure confidence behold him, when he shall come to be our judge; who liveth and reigneth with thee and the Holy Ghost, one God, world without end. *Amen.*

Or,

THE COLLECT FOR CHRISTMAS DAY

ALMIGHTY GOD, who hast given us thy only-begotten Son to take our nature upon him, and as at this time to be born of a pure Virgin: Grant that we being regenerate, and made thy children by adoption and grace, may daily be renewed by thy Holy Spirit; through the same our Lord Jesus Christ, who liveth and reigneth with thee and the same Spirit, ever one God, world without end. *Amen.*

THE BLESSING

MAY he who by his Incarnation gathered into one things earthly and heavenly, fill you with the sweetness of inward peace and goodwill; and the blessing of God Almighty, the Father, the Son, and the Holy Ghost, be upon you and remain with you always. *Amen.*